MIXED

MIXED

NICOLE ZELNIKER

The Nasiona

San Francisco

Mixed

Copyright © Nicole Zelniker, 2019

Published by *The Nasiona*

For information contact:

nasiona.mail.@gmail.com

https://thenasiona.com/

Cover image by Joanna Staniszewski

ISBN: 978-1-950124-01-5

In memory of Jeff Jeske, who shared

his love of journalism with a

freaked-out college first-year. Thank you.

And to my first grade teacher, who thought

I wouldn't amount to anything because

I wouldn't hold a pencil correctly: Ha, ha.

Contents

Foreword

IN THE SUMMER OF 2018, I launched *The Nasiona*, whose mission is to cultivate the seeds of nonfiction. We do this through our magazine, podcast, publishing house, and editing services. Though many in the industry deem us a literary project, I founded *The Nasiona* as an unconventional journalism organization. The former is a means to achieving the latter. I believe objective reporting is a myth, so I embrace the subjectivity of human experience to get a better vantage point of our condition as persons. As a result, though the stories we publish focus on creative works based on facts, truth-seeking, human concerns, real events, and real people, we like to pay attention to more than "just the facts, ma'am."

At *The Nasiona*, we dig deeper into the who and the why than traditional news sources. We look for *why* people are the way they are to better understand *who* they were, are, and want to become. We believe it is in the reformation of these conventional constellations that we can better understand *when* and *how* people behave in a certain way to enact the *what* of their lives depending on where they were, are, and will be.

What drew me to publish Nicole Zelniker's manuscript was that it exemplified what both she and I believe journalism should do: tell stories through us. *Mixed* gives a voice to those who have not traditionally been given a voice in the United States, and, as a result, we are better for it.

This kind of holistic reporting, untethered to the myth of objectivity, adds value to the discourse and the industry in a more authentic way because we deal with honesty and the vulnerabilities of individuals and embrace the fact that our memories and shared histories, our truths and facts, can be limited, distorted, or false, especially if we never engage and speak with the individuals behind the statistics.

Our actions are rooted in the personal narratives we tell ourselves. We live in our heads and our hearts. Thus, it makes sense to excavate those stories to truly catch a glimpse at what makes us tick. It is by getting inside the personal narratives that we can more effectively comprehend why people love and hate, where biases and prejudices are born and nurtured, and what holds us back from developing into who we want to become.

It is these stories that interest me for *The Nasiona*. It is these stories that Zelniker shares in *Mixed*. She introduces us to the people behind the statistics and about what it means to be mixed in the US today.

I believe that searching for, discovering, and promoting such stories helps build bridges between strangers. We tend to be afraid of the unknown and what we don't understand. Fear creates tension, division, and conflict, which can lead to violence. With these stories, I hope to put the overlooked and undervalued up front of people so we can lock eyes with it. In the end, I hope that we can remove a barrier, no matter how small, which may lend to a more harmonious relationship between people, even if they disagree with each other.

I felt the need to create *The Nasiona*—and to publish *Mixed* as our first book under our publishing house—because of my own experiences as a mixed Other and experiences I had working in the space of conflict resolution. I spent many years engaged in trying to understand armed conflict, what pushes people toward violence, what drives fundamentalists, and how we can create lasting, enduring peace in a plural, diverse world.

After the US military denied me acceptance as a teenager because I was not yet a documented migrant, I worked my way into university. I received a BA in philosophy, a BA in communication, and an MA in justice studies from the University of New Hampshire, and I was a PhD candidate at University of British Columbia Okanagan's interdisciplinary graduate studies program, where I focused on political science and Latin American studies.

I've gathered nearly two decades' experience as a journalist, researcher, writer, editor, and educator. I've run several cultural and arts organizations, edited journals and books, was a social justice and public history researcher, taught university courses, and managed a history museum. I've written books and columns on history, culture, and how Othering can guide a people toward armed conflict. I've won grants and fellowships to conduct research in these areas and have given talks at conferences, like the International Congress of the Latin American Studies Association to discuss my work.

My experience leading up to founding *The Nasiona* was that it was very difficult to change people's minds through mere argumentation, which was my preparation as an academic. I was trained to learn as much as I could about a topic and to then propose a well-reasoned argument that may persuade an individual to accept my propositions. Though this obviously works in many cases, it often does not when it comes to intense issues where beliefs and prejudices have grown deep roots. This is especially true for faith-based beliefs, be it political, social, economic, or religious.

Add to the aforementioned a desire for vengeance and the fear of death or loss of liberties, and this tends to be the general outline of most extreme conflicts, like the one I spent years studying and reporting on: the Colombian armed conflict in South America. And with such conflicts follow a wave of propaganda to justify involvement in said conflicts. This only helps the roots of prejudice and hatred grow deeper by creating even larger divides through fomenting fear of the Other—a person or group of people who we view or treat as intrinsically different from and alien to ourselves.

But those who are intrinsically different have a face. A voice. A history. And depending on which camp you reside, you too are the Other. We are all Others. With *The Nasiona*, I want to bridge that divide by humanizing the Other so the Other is no longer just a number, someone who threatens our way of life, but also a human being, flawed and with dreams deserving of respect like the rest of us, like you believe you deserve. I want to give the reader a glimpse into different worlds from our own and, simultaneously, a glimpse into our shared worlds. *Mixed* does that.

During my work leading up to founding *The Nasiona*, I realized that it wasn't simply through argument that most people would open the door to new ideas. For example, if I start a persuasive campaign essentially with "You are wrong and I am right because of a, b, and c," I've already lost most people, even if I presented scientific facts, even if I unearthed logical fallacies. They'd become defensive, and their honor, pride, whatever, would be at stake.

However, if we start simply by sharing personal stories, being vulnerable about who we are and why we are, people tend to abandon their defensive stances even slightly. They are less apt to take to the offensive, and listen. Not only may we learn to see each other as more fully human in this way, but we may begin to no longer see strangers simply as Others, as potential enemies. This shift of engagement opens a space for a potential recognition of the Other's humanity. It creates a potential environment where former enemies may be able speak to or see each other as imperfect humans who act in different ways because of circumstance, genetics, or beliefs.

Sadly people, including myself, don't care as much as we'd like about facts, or we interpret them differently to fit our own narratives about the world. Most of the time we do this subconsciously. So, how do we engage in meaningful dialogue with a perceived enemy or someone we fear or someone who fears or hates us? How do we connect with someone whose very existence challenges you or your worldview?

How we introduce ourselves to others will shape how we engage with the Other, with the stranger, with the unknown, thereby creating a different relationship. This is what I'm trying to do with *The Nasiona* and by publishing Zelniker's *Mixed*. I'm trying to highlight complex stories, but beyond mere statistics.

Not every transformative experience will turn into empathy, and maybe they don't all deserve to, but fully grasping the why and the how is not only a more complete story, but a story that can transform, create humility, construct bridges, cultivate empathy, and produce a situation that may disrupt our personal worlds. This way, we aren't just walking around on autopilot and acting as if everything is merely a black and white issue. I want us to be counted. We've been discounted for far too long.

We live in the gray, in the nuances, in the mixed. I felt the need to shine a spotlight on that arena with more vigor. The individuals with whom Zelniker speaks in each chapter are the kinds of complex, real, and honest characters I grew up wanting to see on the screen and in literature; yet, they are real people. It is these people and their stories I want to introduce.

Though mixed individuals have different stories and come from diverse backgrounds, we are all connected by the experience of living in this liminal space. Every story in *Mixed* felt like it was a part of me, as if it were in my own head, from my own heart. I felt like if people only read this book, they would understand my experience better, an experience I wasn't introduced to at school by teachers, on the field by coaches, or even dissected at home with my family. An experience I had lived, but few understood or even knew existed. Their stories created a bond with me.

To write *Mixed*, Zelniker spoke to dozens of mixed-race families and individuals, as well as experts in the field—such as psychologist Cirleen DeBlaere and historians José Moya and Karl Jacoby—about their own experiences, with the hope to fill a gap in the very important conversation about race. The definition of families is widening, whether it's because of mixed-race relationships, interracial adoption, etc. Today, it is important to hear from a growing population about race, their shifting identities, and what family means to them.

Mixed takes us on a journey and helps us glimpse into overlooked worlds and engage the spectrum of human experience. In doing so, Zelniker and *Mixed* are evidence of one of *The Nasiona*'s strongest pillars: the subjective can offer its own reality and reveal truths some facts cannot discover.

Julián Esteban Torres López

Founder, Executive Director, Editor-in-Chief, *The Nasiona*

San Francisco

Introduction

WILLIAM DANIEL JOHNSON, CHAIRPERSON OF the American Freedom Party, is a white nationalist. In 1985, he authored the "Pace Amendment" under pseudonym James O. Pace in an attempt to repeal the 14th Amendment, which granted freedom to former slaves, and 15th Amendment, which granted black men the right to vote. He has led American Freedom Party conferences, addressed Tea Party conventions, and spoken on CNN. In every case, he has attempted to spread white nationalist ideology. Once, he said that everyone with a drop of black blood should be deported.

In 2016, the Donald Trump administration selected Johnson to be a California delegate. Although the Trump administration has since said it was a mistake to nominate Johnson, it has nonetheless been easier for white nationalists like Johnson, who hopes for his views to become mainstream, to express their ideology since Trump was inaugurated in January 2017.

As one group in the United States continues to become more visible, white supremacists like Johnson will attempt to make their lives more difficult. In 2000, the US census added a mixed-race category, revealing a growing number of mixed-race families. Pew estimates that as many as nearly 7 percent of all adults in the US are now mixed-race or identify themselves as more than one race.

In 2013, 12 percent of newlyweds reported marrying someone of a race they do not identify as. These newlyweds joined the 6.3 percent of all couples in that same year who were part of a mixed-race marriage, according to the Pew Research Center.

In 2015, approximately 14 percent of infants in the US, defined as one year of age or younger, were reported as multiracial or multiethnic. This is close to triple the numbers from 1980, just 35 years prior. The census predicts that by 2060, those numbers will triple once more. Twenty-two percent of multiracial infants have a parent who also identify as multiracial.

Most mixed-race infants come from Hawaii, where 44 percent of infants are multiracial, Oklahoma, where 28 percent are interracial, and Alaska, also 28 percent according to Pew. Nicholas Jones, chief of the US Census Bureau's Racial Statistics Branch, has said that "These comparisons show substantial growth in the multiple-race population, providing detailed insights to how this population has grown and diversified over the past decade."

Ideas of race as a concept are changing, as well. Over the course of history, different races that have been considered white or non-white have switched categories. José Moya, Professor of History at Barnard College, said, "Groups that are now considered whites, such as Jews, Italians, and Irish-Americans, at some point were considered either non-white or an inferior category of white.

Mexicans, on the other hand, were legally defined white for most of the country's history, but are now considered non-whites." Thus, he said, "All of the racial categories used in the US are arbitrary."

Much of the language we use to define racial categories we use interchangeably, even though they mean different things. For example, many of the Hispanic or Latinx people in this book use those words to mean the same thing, even though "Hispanic" means people who come from countries colonized by Spain and "Latinx" means anyone who comes from Latin America, which includes several Portuguese-speaking countries. Many people also use the word "Spanish" to mean Hispanic or Latinx, even though it technically only refers to people from Spain or the Spanish language.

The same is true for the words "Caucasian" and "White" and for the words "African American" and "Black." "Caucasian" technically refers to people from a region in the southeast of Europe, and thus not all white people are Caucasian. The same is true for "African American" and "Black," as not all black people in the US are from Africa.

At the heart of the issue are mixed-race families. Many mixed-race children have had difficulties fitting in, whether with one race or the other. In mixed-race relationships, one partner may face racism, while the other may not, or else they will experience racism in different ways. Children who have been adopted into families that identify as a race that is not theirs often find that they struggle to fit in with their families as well as with people who identify as their own race.

Not only are these families navigating US American culture at large, but they also must navigate their own family structures and what it means to be mixed. The above trends have meant that diversity is increasing within individual families as well as in the US.

Most of the families in this book—and many of the experts—are from New York, where about 3 percent of residents identify as two or more races according to the census, or else members of the families live in New York now. White residents, the state's largest group, have decreased from 95 percent in 1940 to 58 percent in 2010, and it is only going to get smaller, especially as more immigrants of color make their home in the US.

As of 2011, 56 percent of all infants in New York were of color, meaning they were a race that is not white. The second largest population after white in New York is the black population at 16 percent, the second highest in the country after Georgia, although Washington, D.C., where 50 percent of residents are black, has the largest black population relative to its size.

New York's third largest population, Asian, is about 7 percent, the second largest after California, with Hawaii having the largest population for its size, since 57 percent of all Hawaiian residents are Asian. New York is also one of three states, the other two being California and Texas, where the number of mixed-race people exceeded more than half a million, according to the 2010 census data.

Although New York has a long Native American history, specifically Iroquois and Algonquin, the Native American population today is less than 1 percent. The US census does not identify Hispanic or Latinx as a race, but notes that people who identified as such consisted of 18 percent of the population as of 2010.

The families in this book have something in common other than being mixed-race New Yorkers: most of them are part white, part of color. This is because it is not just self-identified white nationalists who are making it difficult for people of color in the US. About 58 percent of white voters helped elect Trump in the 2016 election. One focus of this book is the divides that come from varying levels of privilege.

It is important to note, however, that many mixed-race families are made up of two or more non-white races. Also, most of these families were interviewed in 2017 and 2018, two to three years before the 2020 census and within the first two years of the Trump presidency.

Of the millions of mixed-race families in the US and around the world, the families in this book cannot represent them all. There will be many experiences not told here. These families can only represent themselves and share their own experiences. That said, each and every one of the families interviewed for this book had one thing in common: they do not see themselves as a mixed-race family. They are just family, and they happen to be mixed.

The people interviewed for this book are as follows: Daniela Galimi, who is Dominican and Italian, and who struggles with her identity as mixed-race. She and her mother, Clara Cardiello, are still figuring out what race is together, and what it means to be Dominican in the US.

Helen Sheenan and her two daughters, Joy and Kristen, who do not feel a strong connection to Helen's father's Indian ancestry. While all of them identify more as white than Indian, Helen does hope that her daughters maintain some relationship with that side of their family.

Laura Generale, who feels the tension between her Italian and her Puerto Rican and Spanish sides, though she does think that her parents' cultures come together in a beautiful way.

Jenna Ng Lowry, who has started to care more about her Chinese and white identity as she has gotten older. Her parents,

Delores Ng and Andy Lowry, have always tried to let their daughters know that their Chinese ancestry is important.

Psychologist Cirleen DeBlaere and PhD student Layla

Layla, who can attest to the fact that mixed-race families are often polarized along racial lines, both through their research and their own experiences.

Professor José Moya, a long-time professor of Latin America. In all that time, he's come to the conclusion that race is essentially a meaningless concept.

Nina Werbel Blauner and her husband Sid, both white. They have a biological son Ethan, also white, and an adopted son Zeke, who is black. While life has been different for Ethan and Zeke because of their races, Nina hopes both of her sons can shine.

Gillian Sherman, still struggling with being the only Asian person adopted into an all-white family. Now, she's starting to understand what her Asian identity really means to her, and how it affects her interactions with the world.

Jae Langton, a teenager who does not talk much about race, even though he is South Korean and the rest of his family is white. For his parents, though, adopting a Korean son was a very intentional choice.

Shari Goldstein, the founder of Camp China for Chinese adoptees, her daughter Leah Whetten-Goldstein, adopted from China, and Ecuadorian adoptee Elias Smolcic-Larson.

Media studies professor Trey Ellis, whose family is multiracial. Ellis believes it is important to create diverse casts and that while people identifying as mixed-race are more common in the media than ever, but there's still a long way to go.

Karl Stewart, who is black, and David Pasteelnick, who is white, a married couple from Brooklyn. While they still face both racism and homophobia, they do agree that they have benefitted a lot from the progress made in the last few years.

Lynda Gomi, who is white, and Kazu Gomi, who is Japanese. They have lived in both the US and Japan and both believe that their cultures are a much bigger difference between them than the color of their skin.

Simone Thomas, who is West African, and Alanna Ramos, who is Puerto Rican, both women of color, but who have very different backgrounds. The two of them navigate colorism, cultures, and privilege together.

Julian Humes, who is black, and his girlfriend, Devon Murphy-Anderson, who is white. Though they understand the world very differently, they have spent the last few years learning to understand each other's perspectives.

Professor of history and ethnic studies Karl Jacoby, who believes race is a social construct meant to benefit those with lighter skin and that interracial marriage is not the solution to racism.

While mixed-race families face different challenges than a family of one race would, they face them together. They balance acknowledging their differences with loving each other unconditionally. At a time when racial tensions are rising in the US, it is more important now than ever to listen to stories like these.

Disclaimers

I, NICOLE ZELNIKER, AM NOT MIXED-RACE. I am not biracial, interracial, multiracial, or anything other than a European-American white woman whose family is also very white and European. My great-grandparents come from Austria and Germany. You get the idea.

In January 2017, I co-authored an article about the Muslim community's reaction to the impending Trump presidency. In it, I did what I believe journalism should do: allow people to tell their stories through me. As a graduate student at the Columbia Journalism School, I wanted to delve further into the stories marginalized communities had to tell.

Considering the immigration debate, race had been on the forefront of my consciousness, particularly changing ideas of race. Just last century, Italian and Irish immigrants were considered non-white, or a substandard class of white. Arabs had been considered white until relatively recently, as well. Every time we in the United States get a new flood of immigrants, we change our ideas of race to keep a small, select group of predominantly wealthy white men in charge.

My research began with Google. I found several Pew Research studies about interracial relationships and mixed-race children in the US. Since the 1960s, interracial relationships have risen dramatically, leading to a rise in mixed-race children in the US. According to the US Census Bureau, the number of Americans identifying as mixed race went up 32 percent between 2000 and 2010, and that number will only continue to grow.

What surprised me the most was how willing people were to open themselves up to me. The families I spoke with were brutally honest about their feelings on being mixed or being part of a mixed-race family. Most of the families I spoke with were caught off guard by my request, since they said they thought of themselves as just a family, not necessarily a mixed-race family. There are also many people who are against interracial relationships, and interracial adoption, some of whom I did speak with. I decided against including them in the end. These were not the voices I wanted to highlight here.

In writing this book, I hope to uplift the voices of people in a growing minority group. I thought for a while about writing this book in first person, since most of what I learned, I learned from extensive and personal interviews with gracious people sharing their stories with me. I quickly decided that would be a terrible idea. The point of this book is not to talk about my relationships with my interviewees. It is to talk about these individuals and families' day to day experiences being who they are, and in that I have no place. In fact, this and the acknowledgements, located at the very end of the book, will be the only places where you will have to hear from me in first person.

Most of the names in this book are real, though some have been changed upon the interviewees' requests. The rest of the information—age, gender, race, etc.—has not been changed.

Some of the people in this book I've met recently. With David and Karl, I reached out to them through Facebook because of a *Huffington Post* article in which David spoke about Loving Day. I was very lucky in that I met two people who were open to having a conversation with a stranger about their marriage. Others, like the Langtons, I've known since I was five years old, when Rachael Langton and I were in the same kindergarten class at Concord Road Elementary School in Ardsley, New York. In every situation, the people I spoke to were incredibly open to talking about their lives and receptive to my many questions. For that, I am eternally grateful.

Mixed

Part One

"We are family."–Sister Sledge, a US American music group

CHAPTER ONE

"Why is There No Mixed for Me?"

From the Pew Research Center: Sixty percent of mixed-race adults in the US are proud of their backgrounds.

DANIELA GALIMI, 19, WANTS TO TEACH. As an education major at Keene State College, she has already spent a year as a student teacher in New Hampshire public schools. However, her biggest lesson so far may be that even among her students, she is thought of as different.

"It's really tough being in the schools," said Daniela. "The kids did a family tree, and we all had to bring in pictures of our parents, so I did it with them. They were in awe that my mom looked the way she did and my dad looked the way he did."

Daniela is one of nine million people in the United States who identify as mixed-race according to information from the 2010 US census. Her mother, Clara Cardiello, is Dominican and her father, Edward Galimi, is Italian and Irish. When Clara and Edward married in in the 1990s, they were among 964,000 other multiracial newlyweds in the US, just under 2 percent of all married couples.

According to a Pew Research Center Report published in 2015, that number has risen dramatically in the past few years. In 2013, 12 percent of newlyweds reported marrying someone of a different race, making the total number of interracial couples in the US just over 6 percent. Between 2000 and 2010, the number of mixed-race people in the US grew by 32 percent. For comparison, those who identified as one race grew just over 9 percent.

In turn, the percentage of multiracial infants is also on the rise. According to the same Pew report, it was approximately 14 percent in 2013, close to triple the share of 1980 births.

There are flaws in the study—for example, it only counted infants from two-parent households—meaning the number of mixed-race babies born in the US is actually likely to be higher than the official reports indicate.

This is a significant demographic shift, and it shows no signs of slowing down. For now, people like Daniela, who identify as more than one race, navigate their identities with little guidance other than a constant stream of conflicting opinions about what it means and who they are.

Daniela spent most of her childhood in Mineola, a village on Long Island that has a large white majority. In the 2010 census, over 71 percent of Mineola residents identified as non-Hispanic white and about 16 percent as Hispanic or Latinx, which is the gender-neutral version of Latino or Latina. The census uses non-Hispanic white because Hispanic and Latinx are identified as an ethnicity on the census, not a race, and therefore Hispanic people are often counted as white or black. Only 2 percent of Mineola residents identified as more than one race.

"It kind of puts pressure on you," said Daniela. "Everyone kind of has to act Americanized, so to speak. Me and my sister and one other boy were the only Spanish kids in our class. I remember coming home one day after my class found out I was Spanish, that I was different. I was mortified."

Because she looks more like her Dominican mother, with dark, curly hair, brown eyes, and darker skin, many people assume Daniela is Hispanic at first. But when they learn that her surname is Italian, they do a double-take and conclude she must be white.

Even with her friends, whether Hispanic or white, Daniela feels out of place. "My fully Spanish friends will be like, 'You're half white. You don't get it.' And then my fully white friends will be like, 'You're Spanish, you don't get it,'" she said. "I'm either 100 percent white or I'm 100 percent Spanish. It's so frustrating."

The situation gets still more complicated when people find out that, unlike about two-thirds of the 50 million Hispanics in the US, Daniela doesn't speak Spanish. She said that as an education major, it would have been very helpful to know another language, or even to know more about another culture when dealing with her students. Of not learning another language, she said, "I regret it so much."

Keene, New Hampshire, where Daniela attends college, had an estimated population of 23,406 in 2016 and is even less diverse than Mineola. Over 95 percent of residents in Keene identify as white, less than 2 percent as Hispanic, and less than 2 percent as multiracial.

At Keene State College, which had a total enrollment of 4,165 students as of 2016, or about one-fifth of the town's population, no one really knows what to do about a multiracial student, particularly one who has an Italian surname but whose brown eyes, curly dark hair, and dark skin identify her as Hispanic.

"When I was signing up to be an education major, my advisor asked me, 'Okay, what are you,'" said Daniela. "I said, 'I'm half white and I'm half Hispanic.' She asked me, 'Do you speak Spanish?' I said no. And she checked off 'white.'"

According to College Factual, which tracks student demographic information such as race, white students make up 85 percent of the school, while nearly 4 percent are Hispanic or Latinx. There are more students of unknown ethnicity at Keene State College, about 8 percent, than there are any individual minority groups.

Daniela does think, however, that the non-white students she has met at Keene are much more open about expressing their cultures, specifically through their clothes, than they were at her high school, where "It wasn't accepted as much," said Daniela. "You would never guess that half of my friends then weren't from this country. They had to dress like the white Americans dress."

* * *

On a cold December day, Daniela and her mother sat in the Starbucks on Central Avenue in Westchester County, where Leona Lewis, a biracial singer from London, played over the speakers and blenders whirred in the background. Three other customers tapped away on their computer keyboards. A self-professed Starbucks addict, Daniela said her affinity for the coffee corporation is one of the many things about her that makes her "Americanized."

Soon, Clara would return to her job as a program coordinator for Knowing Science in Armonk, New York. Armonk is located in North Castle, which is 92 percent white, 4 percent Hispanic and Latinx, and less than 2 percent mixed-race. Though she had already been to work that day, Clara had to return that evening for a second shift.

Having a Dominican mother and an Italian father, Clara said, was a non-issue when Daniela and her sisters, twin Briana and older sister Ariella, were growing up, since that was all they had ever known.

"Coming from a mixed family, it was just normal," Clara said. "It was normal for their mom to be Spanish and it was normal for their dad to be white." It wasn't until they went to school that Clara's daughters found out they were different from the other students there, most of whom were white.

"They were being exposed to that at a very young age," she continued. "And then moving into the middle school and high school, because of all the neighborhoods were merged, that's when they were exposed to more of the Spanish culture or the Spanish population that was in the neighborhood. It's a very small one, but it was the first time they didn't feel like the odd ones out. There were other people that looked a little more like them."

Clara, who divorced Daniela's father many years ago, is the child of two immigrants from the Dominican Republic. "Growing up, if anybody asked me, I would say I'm Spanish, and my mom would always correct me," she said. "She would say, 'No, you're American.'"

Clara's parents brought her up in a Spanish-speaking home in Jamaica, Queens. Although she wanted to teach her daughters Spanish when she became a mother herself, she never did so.

"I think maybe if I would have married someone who was Spanish, I probably would have gone a different route," she said. "My oldest daughter has a speech disability, so once she started going into speech therapy, they told me I had to stick to one language."

Because her parents only spoke Spanish when they came to the US, Clara's first language is Spanish. She did not learn English until she began attending kindergarten with English-speaking children.

"I was brought up with the culture, but with the kids, we don't do a lot of traditional, even foods and stuff like that," said Clara. "Like, Christmas, when I was little, we would celebrate Christmas Eve. That's more Spanish. Once I had the kids, I started celebrating Christmas Day. Just little things like that."

Language is only one of the many differences in Clara's upbringing and that of her own children. After her divorce, she married another white man, a choice she said stems from her first boyfriend, who was Dominican, having cheated on her.

"Dominican men are known to be players," she said. "I guess, because of that, it kind of implanted in my head. I guess I dated more white men than Spanish, especially as I got older." She added, "When I was younger, I used to say all the time, I'm going to marry a blond man with blue eyes. And funnily enough, their father is blond with blue eyes."

Daniela has also dated people of various races, including white and Hispanic. She said that the longest relationship she's ever been in was with a white boy.

"After that, it was Spanish, then black, and now, someone who's half Spanish and half white, like me," she said. "When I was with the black guy, he was like, 'Oh, I like you because you're different.' And I was like, 'What do you mean, I'm different?' And he'd be like, 'Well, we're in New Hampshire.' And I would always get so bothered by that. It's not that different. I'm just a little darker than all the people here."

In both dating and friendships, Daniela said people make comments on her skin color. "People call me coffee," she said.

"Someone used to call you—what was it? Mocha," Clara added.

Daniela nodded. "People used to give me, like, food nicknames," she said.

Clara said she considers herself lucky in terms of the families of men she's dated, as few of them were racist toward her or disapproved of her because she is Hispanic. "I did encounter it with a boyfriend, someone I dated in college, and funnily enough, they were Spaniards," she said. "But, they were European and lily white. My grandfather is from Spain. So if you saw my dad, you would think he was white. My mom is very dark, much darker than me, so I'm kind of like a mix of the two of them. With that situation, the parents were like, 'Well we can kind of accept her, but the fact that the mother's so dark, you know ...'" Clara trailed off and then said, "That was a huge issue for them."

Hispanic as a category has always been tricky. Legally, the US census has categorized Hispanic as an ethnicity and not a race.

However, according to José Moya, the Institute of Latin American Studies program director at Barnard College, changing demographics have led to changing ideas of race. He said that because the Hispanic population in the US has grown so large, experts are starting to reconsider what it means to be Hispanic.

For Daniela, this makes her identity even more complicated. Not only is she struggling with what her race is, but also with being more than one race.

"Everyone always makes jokes about it," said Daniela. "I'm always the one that's made fun of. People make jokes, especially at the school I'm in now, because we're in New Hampshire.

"When we take tests, there's always white, black, Spanish, other," she added. "Why is there no mixed for me?"

CHAPTER TWO

Can I Get a Nose Ring?

From the US Census Bureau: In 2010, 16 states had more than 200,000 people who identified as mixed-race.

VERY RARELY DOES HELEN SHEENAN, 54, tell people who aren't Indian that her father was from India. With her light skin and light brown hair, she more closely resembles her white mother, and she did not experience a lot of Indian culture growing up in the US. "If I meet a white person, it usually doesn't come up unless they ask," she said.

The question of background most often comes up if she mentions her maiden name, which is the Indian surname Das. "It's a very unusual spelling, so then, white people will ask me, but normally, I don't really get into that," she said.

As of the 2010 census, approximately 1.6 million US Americans identify as Asian and white, like Helen. The population of biracial Asian and white Americans grew 87 percent between 2000 and 2010, or by 750,000 people. The only faster-growing group was biracial black and white Americans, which increased by 134 percent or 1 million people over that same period, and of which there are now 1.8 million total.

Also like Helen, many biracial US Americans identify more with one race than the other. In her case, she identifies as mostly white, although on official forms, "I check off the box that says two or more races, and it has in parenthesis, South Pacific Islander, Asian, whatever."

Helen grew up in Rochester, New York, which at the time was 81 percent white and only 2 percent Asian, and as a child she spent far more time with her white mother than her Indian father, who was away at work all day as an engineer. Her family later moved to Washington, D.C., where Helen attended middle and high school, which is nearly 35 percent non-Hispanic white and 4 percent Asian. The largest population, black, is just over 50 percent.

"If you're mixed-race and you have a strong culture of one of those races, I think it makes it easier to identify as that race," she said. "I was more raised by my mom, who was white. So I think I identify more as white, but if I had more Indian family, maybe I would have identified more as Indian. My mom was actually more involved in trying to make sure I knew about my Indian background than my dad was.

"If we had had Indian family here, maybe we would have celebrated Diwali and those kinds of holidays," she added. "But because my family in Rochester was all Caucasian and Christian, we celebrated their holidays."

Helen's father, who died about 20 years ago, came to the US to attend George Washington University in Washington, D.C., where he met Helen's mother. "He came here for education," said Helen. "He came here for a job. He completed all his studies in India and he got his master's or bachelor's of science in chemistry. And he got into school over here, so he came here."

After he met Helen's mother, Helen's father broke off the arranged marriage that was scheduled for his return to India, which Helen's daughter Joy said reminds her of the plot of the movie, *The Big Sick*, where Kumail Nanjiani's character, who is from Pakistan, refuses to marry anyone from Pakistan after he falls in love with a white woman from the US.

"They met because my mom was the president of the international relations club," Helen said. "And my dad went to some meetings, and that's how he met her. Back then, because he had a brother and a sister, his family could only afford to send one, and he was the oldest boy, so he's the one who got sent."

Helen and her daughter Joy both ended up going to George Washington University for college, as well. The school is about 56 percent white and 10 percent Asian.

"My father didn't really embrace his roots," said Helen. "He wanted to be Westernized. He thought, if you're going to come to a place, then you need to be like the people who are here, instead of trying to have your culture."

Helen herself has never dated any Indian men. "The Indians who were here had very strong connections with other Indians," she said. "They do things socially, and I think that's how they meet people. My dad wasn't a part of that culture here, so I never met any Indian guys here. Although, I think my aunt offered when I visited to have an arranged marriage for me." She laughed at the recollection.

* * *

Helen lives with her daughters, Joy, 22, and Kristen, 19, and her husband, Philip, in their house in Hartsdale, New York, where the population is about 76 percent white and about 10 percent Asian or Pacific Islander. About 2 percent of people living there are mixed-race, according to the census.

Helen and Philip, who is white, have lived in Hartsdale since Joy and Kristen were children. Joy and Kristen identify strongly as white, their Indian grandfather having died when Joy was three years old and Kristen was only a baby. Helen mentioned that her father wanted to name the girls "Brittney or something," since he wanted them to be very American.

Like Daniela Galimi, Helen and Joy aren't entirely sure what they believe race is. The two of them sat in their living room downstairs with their chocolate lab, Gus, waiting for Kristen to join them.

"I guess your genetic background," Helen said, scratching Gus behind the ears. "I don't know, your genetic makeup."

"Just like your color?" Joy asked. "Or —"

"No, not your color, because you can be Caucasian and dark-skinned," Helen amended. "Race and color of skin don't necessarily coincide. I would say it's your genetics, whatever your DNA is, whatever genetic roots you come from."

"I guess," Joy said. "Well, what's the difference between race and ethnicity?"

"Well, ethnicity is what your culture is."

"Okay, yeah, I guess that's fair," Joy said. "Yeah, then I guess it's just your genetic makeup. I mean, literally, I guess that's what it is, but I guess it has connotations about your culture also."

Although Helen does not identify as much with Indian culture, Joy said that Helen does get excited when she meets another Indian person. "You ask them where they're from, make that connection with them, and they open up a little bit," she said.

"Right, that camaraderie or whatever that is," Helen added.

Joy also thinks her mother is happy when she befriends other Indian women. "Like Ramya, Minal," Joy said, listing her Indian friends. "You were happy when Kristen made a friend at school named Meena, whose family is from India. Like, you were so happy to talk to their parents about where your father is from."

"Yeah," Helen said. "I mean, I think it's good. Even though you're two generations down the line, I'm happy that you have people that you know that remind you of that culture and remind you that this is part of your identity, too."

"And I think also, you adopted a lot of the way your father raised you into how you raise us," said Joy. "And you think that Indian parents know what they're doing because they don't let their kids mess around."

"It's much stricter," Helen said. "Now, as an adult, I appreciate that."

At school, Joy said she naturally gravitated toward students of Indian descent. "I think there are a lot of international students at GW, especially from India," she said. "In my first year, most of my friends were international. My first two years I was definitely quieter, didn't really go out to parties, just wanted to stay in and study and focus on my grades, and that's how I found my close friends from that year.

"My friend Ramya, it was her first time spending a long time in the US coming from a stricter home life in India," she added. "And then my friend and my roommate Maya, her parents were from Indian descent and I think her father is from Malaysia or something. So just by nature of who I was and how I was raised, that's what drew me to this close group of friends that were kind of like that. I'm just saying, sometimes it's hard to find that commonality with my friends who—"

"—have white parents," Helen finished.

Joy nodded. "Yeah. I mean, I don't really think I was conscious about it as a cultural thing. I think I knew you were different from other people's parents, but I don't think it was until I was in college that I realized that Maya's parents were kind of the same way. Maya's parents were even stricter than you were, because I remember talking to you about things her dad would say to her. Like, he would make her delete a picture off her Facebook. And it wasn't anything racy."

"Oh, it's funny, because that's what my dad would have said to me," Helen said.

Recently, Kristen has been asking her mother if she can get a nose ring, saying that she can because she is a woman of color.

"I think it's just a joke," said Joy about the nose ring. "Because Kristen—"

"No, I think she really wants a nose ring."

"She does really want a nose ring, but the joke is that you look at Kristen and, like, technically, she's got the blood, but she's not a woman of color, you know," Joy said. "It's the same with me, but Kristen is like, 'Oh, I'm a woman of color in STEM.'"

Kristen came downstairs wearing University of Michigan sweatshirt, even though she is a sophomore at Cornell University, where about 41 percent of students are white and 18 percent are Asian. Cornell is ranked high in ethnic diversity, especially for a predominantly white college.

"Kristen, why do you want a nose ring?" Helen asked.

"She just wants it because it looks cool," Joy said. "All of her friends are Asian and Indian anyway."

"I told her that was cultural appropriation," said Helen.

"Which doesn't make sense because it's our culture," said Kristen.

"Well, white women, I mean, look back and the people who colonized the states," said Helen. "None of those women had nose rings. So, none of the European settlers had nose rings, but Asian women had nose rings."

"At this point, I think there's certain things that are clearly a rip-off of their culture, but I don't think just a nose piercing is a rip-off of anyone's culture," said Joy.

"Well, see, I do, because the European white women who came here never wore nose rings, and I think they're stealing it from the Asian women who come here," said Helen. "And Kristen was like, well, technically I am Asian."

"I think with Kristen, it's just more of a joke, because you would look at her and you would never believe it," said Joy.

Kristen nodded. "No one believes it," she said.

Helen went to India for the first time in her twenties. Joy and Kristen both went more recently, in 2016.

"When we were there for just a week, we saw three cities, but we didn't see anywhere where your family was from," Joy said. "We just saw the tourist-y sights, but your family helped show us around."

"But over there they didn't really consider you to be part-Indian," said Helen, as Kristen retreated to her room.

"No, they didn't," Joy said.

"We were at a couple of tourist sights, and especially Kristen, they thought she was an oddity," said Helen.

"A princess." Helen and Joy both laughed.

"Yeah," said Helen. "They surrounded her and started taking photographs of her and wanted to take pictures with her and wanted to touch her hair."

"But, I mean, I didn't feel any type of connection," Joy said. "It was really interesting to see, but I wasn't like, oh, I'm in touch with my roots right now. Because I feel like I don't really have those roots."

CHAPTER THREE

Family Lingers

From the US Census Bureau: In Delaware, Georgia, Kentucky,
Mississippi, North Carolina, South Carolina, South Dakota,
Tennessee, and West Virginia, the mixed-race population grew by
70 percent or more between 2000 and 2010.

AT 23, LAURA GENERALE LEFT QUEENS, where she did
AmeriCorps at a middle school in Astoria the previous year. Her
destination: Long Island, where she attends medical school at Stony
Brook University. Almost 36 percent of the undergraduate students
at Stony Brook are white and 11 percent are Hispanic or Latinx.

It wasn't something she was looking for when she
committed to Stony Brook, but diversity is something that Laura,
who is Puerto Rican, Spanish, and Italian, cares about deeply. At
least, it started to be when Laura went away to college at Cornell
University in 2013. Laura was a senior at Cornell the same year that

Kristen Sheenan was a freshman. Nearly 13 percent of students at Cornell are Hispanic or Latinx.

"I never really thought about having a different upbringing than other people because of my culture or my background," said Laura. "It didn't come up. You don't really discuss that very much. I hit college and I realized I'm not that similar to many people. I didn't realize that my upbringing was that different."

"When I got to school, at the beginning, I was hanging out with more white people, and then I started making more and more Latina friends, and we would discuss that stuff," she added. "I realized there was more connection there.

"College was also when I also really interacted with the real WASP-y whites, which was crazy, because that was just a culture clash in and of itself," Laura said. "To the point where it was difficult for me to talk to some people because I don't think they understood where I was coming from." Now, she said that she chooses to hang out "More with Hispanic people, Hispanic culture, because I'm more familiar with that and I'm more comfortable with that."

In addition to finding that her race plays a part in her friendships, Laura also admitted she thinks it seeps into her dating life, as well.

"Yes, I'm Hispanic, and I'll be able to relate somewhat, but I maybe won't be Spanish enough for guys that are looking for the full-bred Latina. So, I'm always looking out for the tall blonds of the world." She laughed. And then she said, "There's still an interesting dynamic that sometimes I'm hesitant to admit."

Laura grew up with her mother Nancy, her father Piero, and her older brother Adam in Dobbs Ferry, New York, which is nearly 81 percent white, including those who identify as Hispanic and white. All people who identify as Hispanic make up 7 percent of the population according to the 2010 census. For a long time, Nancy's mother, who was Puerto Rican, lived with the family, as well.

For the last year, Laura has lived with her cousin Dani Strigi, a junior at New York University, and a friend from college Ashley Shim, also in the AmeriCorps program. They were able to live in Astoria, which is 49 percent white and 27 percent Hispanic, because Laura and Dani's grandmother, Piero's mother, left their family her house when she passed away.

"My grandmother was not very into the idea, when my dad and my mom were first together," said Laura of her Italian grandmother. "She would make comments, even when I was a kid. But I don't think she made the connection, because I was her granddaughter and I had light skin, that I would internalize it like that." According to Laura, her grandmother would say things like, "Spanish people smell up the church. Spanish people just smell, Laura, they just smell" when Laura and her mother were around. Laura and Nancy would often exchange uncomfortable looks, but would not say anything out loud.

Although Laura became more aware of what race meant to her in college, she was exposed to racism through her family at an early age. "There's a lot of uppity-ness in my household around Italian culture," she said. "It's the 'superior culture' according to my Italian family, so I think I just react differently and take a step back sometimes instead." Plus, Laura joked, she likes the food on her Hispanic side better anyway.

Like Daniela Galimi, Laura did not grow up learning Spanish. However, Laura had the opportunity to learn when her grandmother, her mother's mother, moved in with them after being diagnosed with Alzheimer's. Laura was in middle school at the time.

"My mom basically never spoke Spanish," Laura said. "She would speak with my grandmother, but with my dad, she would only speak English because he doesn't speak Spanish. Growing up, I never really heard Spanish around the house unless Abuela was there.

"The only reason I have a pretty good Spanish-speaking ability now is because Abuela came to live with me from middle school into high school, and she only spoke Spanish at that point," she continued. "The only way I could communicate with her was learning Spanish. And now I've gotten to use it."

Growing up, since Laura's parents did not speak a common language besides English, she said they never thought to teach her another language, whether Spanish or Italian.

"There's this really cool study that says if your mom speaks their native language while you're in the womb, you'll have a preference for that language," said Laura. With her grandmother, "I was exposed to it, but it's not like my mom taught me when I was younger. But she taught my brother, which is kind of messed up," she joked. "Like, c'mon, how unfair is that?"

Laura's maternal grandmother is from San Juan, the capital of Puerto Rico, and her maternal grandfather is from Spain. Laura said her grandfather lived in other countries before coming to the US, like Argentina, after leaving Spain. For a while, he was married to a woman in Brazil and had a daughter with her. Eventually, he ended up on a ship to New York at the same time as Laura's grandmother, who was immigrating to the Bronx.

Laura and her family loved Abuela, even if it was hard for Laura to communicate at first. In fact, Laura said, she would talk about her grandmother all the time.

"I would tell stories about Abuela, which were hilarious," said Laura. "But whenever I got to certain aspects of Hispanic culture or tried to explain some stuff, I could feel people's eyes glazing over, so I thought they couldn't relate to it."

This feeling remains true for many other topics, as well. "When I hang out with my white friends, there are certain things I can't really talk about," said Laura. "Or if I did, I just felt like I was over-explaining and people would just get lost or disinterested."

* * *

Like many people, Laura believes that race is a social construction. "From a biological standpoint, I don't think it exists," she said. "Whenever people refer to it, they're referring to our appearances and color."

She added, "I personally think race has to do a lot with culture, as well. It's something we constructed. So, if you look at it from that school of thought, it's way more culturally based, but I think a lot of people think it's more appearance."

In the US census, Hispanic and Latinx are defined as ethnicities, not races, making it difficult for many people who identify as Hispanic to figure out where they belong. Because Laura is Hispanic and white, she believes she does not have that problem.

"I think there's some debate about whether Hispanic is actually a race, so I always put down on job applications white/Hispanic," said Laura, meaning she marks "white" as her race and "Hispanic" as her ethnicity. "I'm obviously super blanquita. Like, I'm super light-skinned, so I wouldn't say I'm a woman of color. I'm basically half-half.

"I do think, though, that having the experience of coming from a Hispanic background is different from coming from some sort of white background," she noted. "To be honest, I always flip-flop. I would say that being Hispanic is a different experience, feeling more of an other-ness from white people rather."

Because Laura has light brown hair, green eyes, and pale skin, she is often identified as simply "white" before people know she is also Hispanic. Also like Daniela Galimi, her surname, Generale, is Italian. She falls in with the 24 percent of biracial US Americans who feel they have had unfair assumptions made about their race, according to Pew.

This past year, Laura worked at a school in Queens where she taught predominantly black and Hispanic children. Although she would tell them that she was Hispanic and white, she was often frustrated by her students' reactions.

"It's so difficult to deal with because even when I'm talking to my kids about what race means and about what Hispanic means, they're like, 'You're not white, you're Hispanic,'" she said.

Because Hispanic and Latinx culture in the US is so broad, Laura said she struggles to relate to her kids culturally, even though they are also Hispanic.

"I don't know anything about Mexican culture," she said. "And my kids, they're all Mexican. So, I definitely wish I had been exposed to more of that. Even now, I feel pretty lost. I feel like it would've been easier if I had been exposed to that diversity early on." Her Spanish-speaking ability did help her, though. She said, "I made an active effort in college to keep up with Spanish. I did a Spanish minor and now I use it with my kids."

Although Laura has white and Hispanic friends, she said she struggles in both groups, either because there are things she can't talk about regarding Hispanic culture with her white friends or because she feels judged among her Hispanic friends.

"There's the idea of not being Spanish enough. Like, you don't eat platanos all the time," she joked. "Particularly being white and Hispanic, my skin is very light. So, whenever I tell people, they don't believe me. So, I'm trying to prove myself to these people. It's just a weird competition where your Spanish-speaking abilities also come into play."

She added, "I feel more judged on the Hispanic side, and on the white side I just feel out of place sometimes." Among either group, Laura said, "It becomes kind of a burden because I don't get to share everything about my background."

Even in the Spanish language, Laura feels like an outsider. Although she speaks it well, she isn't a fluent bilingual speaker. So much of her identity is about being stuck in the middle. With her parents, however, she feels right at home.

"In some ways, it's interesting because they blend very well," Laura said of Italian and Hispanic culture. "Like, I think my dad and my mom get along so well because of the fact that they're two cultures that rely a lot on Catholicism and religion and the same values of food and family."

CHAPTER FOUR

From New York to Hong Kong

From the Pew Research Center: Fifty-nine percent of mixed-race adults in the US say their identities make them more open to other cultures.

GROWING UP IN ARDSLEY, NEW YORK, where 78 percent of the population is white and 17 percent is Asian, Jenna Ng Lowry never thought her mixed-race background was at all unusual. Jenna, 22, has a white father and a Chinese mother.

"Ardsley, it is very white, but after white, Asian is definitely the highest population," Jenna said on a winter afternoon at her parents' suburban home in Ardsley. Her straight, black hair was tied back as she cooked stir-fry vegetables and tofu for her father, Andy Lowry, 60, and her mother, Delores Ng, 56.

"And, also, mixed-race Asian and white families are very, very common in this area," Jenna added. "And because I went to

Chinese school and there were many families there like that, as well, it just didn't seem out of the norm."

In the fall of 2013, Jenna went to Muhlenberg College, which is in Allentown, Pennsylvania, and is 78 percent white and 3 percent Asian. The town itself is 43 percent non-Hispanic white and 2 percent Asian.

"I remember, in my orientation group, I'd be like, 'Okay, I can look around and see that I am the only person of color here,'" she said. "And all the friends I made were all white girls. It's not like I meant to do that, but I ended up in this group where there's no diversity in it."

The family sat at the dining room table, where Jenna served the stir-fry. "I went to a meeting about financial aid," said Delores about when Jenna first went to college. At the meeting, Delores mentioned to a financial counselor that he should give Jenna aid because the school was so white.

"I said to the guy, you know, 'It's really in your best interest, because if you look around here, it's completely homogeneous, and it would be in your best interest to have someone who's non-white,'" she said. "So, we got the financial aid." Everyone laughed.

"Muhlenberg has been getting more diverse," Jenna conceded. "And I also got more involved in conversations about diversity."

Jenna majored in theater and, in the summer of 2015, worked on a show called the Sedehi Diversity Project that is based on the lives of members of the campus community. Jenna said that working on the show made her think about race for the first time.

"It's more of an issue than I realized growing up," she said. "The Diversity Project shocked me into realizing how white the community was."

That same summer, Donald Trump announced his bid for the presidency of the US, and the topic of race and being multiracial has been on Jenna's mind ever since. Among other things, Trump has gone after Asian trade partners by mimicking stereotypical speech patterns. In 2015, CNN reported that he became frustrated in negotiations with Japan and China as trade partners and said, "When these people walk into the room, they don't say, 'Oh hello, how's the weather? It's so beautiful outside. How are the Yankees doing? They're doing wonderful, that's great.' They say, 'We want deal.'" He placed emphasis on the word "deal," drawing attention to the fact that he had used improper English.

Additionally, *The Huffington Post* reported that hate crimes against Asian Americans surged after Trump declared China an enemy during his campaign. In Los Angeles, California, for example, where 11 percent of the population is Asian, 2015 hate crimes against Asian Americans tripled from the year before.

"It's just constant," she said. "And when the election happened, I was in my suite with a bunch of friends who were over and we were all watching the results come in together and feeling more stressed." By this time, Jenna said, her group of friends had become significantly more diverse.

"There's sometimes when he talks about China and Asia that's just so unnerving," Delores added.

Although she said she does not identify more with either side, Jenna does acknowledge that her identity as a person of color is more visible than her whiteness. "I think that living in America, the side of me that's more noticeable is that I'm Asian," she said. "Because people look at me and the thing that's out of the norm is that I'm not fully white, so that part of my identity is kind of dismissed. But, culturally, I just feel like I'm American."

She gestured toward her father. "We've gotten into some arguments recently, because I feel like I remind my dad that he's a straight, white man. And that there are things that are just more upsetting when you're not, but I think that there are lots of people in my position that don't feel like they can have those conversations with their parents. I have friends who wouldn't feel safe challenging their parents on anything like that, but I know I can."

When they became parents, first to Jenna's older sister Lindsay, 26, and then to Jenna, neither parent thought it would be a problem to raise mixed-race children.

"Mixed-race, Asian and white, seems far less challenging in America than, for instance, mixed-race including black or Hispanic," Andy said. "I don't know exactly why that is, but that's just the way America seems to be. More accepting of Asians than blacks or Hispanics by and large."

"I think I knew a lot of people that had gotten together who were white and Asian, so it just seemed sort of like a common thing," Delores added. "It didn't seem that unusual. I guess, choosing to have kids, the only thing we really thought of were the names. I decided to keep my maiden name, so I played around with the idea that maybe they would take my name, or eventually drop Lowry and just keep Ng, because I gave them Ng as a middle name."

Jenna laughed. "You want me to drop Lowry?"

"Because you figured, at some point, you would probably drop me, right?" Andy joked.

"No," Delores said, also laughing. "I just thought—it was very important for me to give them Ng as a middle name."

* * *

Andy is from upstate New York, which he said is "a very homogenous white population." Delores was born in Hong Kong and raised in the Bronx. For both of them, the reality and implications of being a multiracial family have been part of their lives for decades, especially for Delores. Of Delores's four sisters, two of them are also married to white men, while two of them are married to Asian men. Her only brother is currently dating a white woman.

"We were the first to get married, but the dating had already begun," said Andy. He turned to Delores. "Was it difficult for your parents the first time? When someone was dating non-Chinese?"

Delores shook her head. "No," she said. "I remember my mother saying to me, 'I would prefer you to be with somebody Chinese, but, if you have to go outside of that, then it's okay for him to be white'. Because she basically said, you know, there's a hierarchy, and white people are actually better than Chinese people, but blacks and Hispanics are way below Chinese. So, I guess it was okay to marry up, but not down." Delores shook her head at the memory.

Growing up in the Bronx, which is less than 5 percent Asian, Delores was the only Asian student in her school. "All of us were teased mercilessly," she said. "It was even physical bullying. I remember this kid that would sit across from me and just pinch me under the table. Our friends were black and Hispanic because that was who we were with, but my parents still had this racist attitude that we couldn't really mix with them or something.

"My junior high school graduation, I posed for a photo with my good friend Daryl, who's black, and my mother went ballistic," she added. "It was because the one other Chinese girl from that class, her mother said something. I wasn't making out with him. It was a picture. That was one of the worst moments. I was really just so disappointed in my mother."

Delores and Andy both speak Cantonese, the official language of Hong Kong, Singapore, and Malaysia, and it was important to Delores that her daughters maintain a Chinese identity, so she sent them both to Chinese school as children. But there was a problem: the school taught Mandarin, the official language of mainland China and Taiwan, instead of Cantonese. As a result, Lindsay and Jenna often came home frustrated with their homework, and their parents were unable to help them because they did not speak the language.

"Yeah, it does feel like we put them through something because they really didn't want to," Delores said about Chinese school. "It was Saturday mornings from ten to 12, and for much of the time, I was the most enthusiastic because there was a whole social network there. So, I met all these parents. But the girls, we couldn't really help them."

"And all the homework came back as written Chinese," Andy added. "Pretty much all the other kids got help at home with the homework."

Lindsay ended up taking several semesters of Mandarin at college—"to our surprise," Delores noted—but Jenna went into theater and left the language behind, especially since her theater program at the Broadway Training Center was at the same time as Chinese school. "I know Mandarin is useful in the world, but at age seven, I didn't care about that," she said. "So, I went to Chinese school, but I still couldn't talk to my grandparents or anything like that. So, it wasn't useful, and I ended up dropping it."

Delores nodded. "My parents don't speak English," she said. "Even though we've been here, oh my God, almost 50 years."

After Delores's mother retired, she began taking English lessons, "But it was kind of hopeless" according to Delores. "It's kind of crazy that you're in a country for 50 years and you cannot speak the language," she added. "It was pride, mostly, that my father didn't want to learn the language."

"Jenna would sometimes sit with her for an hour or so," Andy added about Jenna's grandmother.

"Every so often," said Jenna.

"That's why I actually tried to study some," Andy said of communicating with his in-laws. "I learned some Cantonese where I can actually understand a fair amount of what's discussed. I can only respond in very simple ways, but it's something."

"I always say she should have just raised me bilingual," Jenna said of Delores. "Because if there was the opportunity to raise your children bilingual, why wouldn't you take it? They use Cantonese when they don't want the kids to know what they're saying, now. Lindsay and I know nothing."

"No, they know the foods," Delores said. For Jenna, she said, this is the most important part.

CHAPTER FIVE

'Me'Search

From the Mixed Remixed: Psychologists have said there are many advantages to identifying as mixed-race.

THE HIGHLY POLARIZED POLITICAL ATMOSPHERE in the US has exacerbated the divides for many mixed-race families. Layla Rafaoui, a US American student at Trinity College in Dublin, Ireland, comes from one such family. Layla, who is Swedish on her mother's side and Moroccan on her father's side, is studying for her PhD in International Conflict with a focus on interfaith marriages in a city that is 90 percent white and 1 percent black.

Her experiences being mixed-race, as well as Jewish and Muslim, she said, have contributed to her desire to study international conflict. Pew estimates that 45 percent of Jews and 21 percent of Muslims live with a romantic partner that identified as a faith that was not the other person's.

The number of interfaith marriages has escalated in recent years aside the number of mixed-race marriages, from 19 percent before the 1960s to 39 percent between 2010 and 2015. Forty-nine percent of unmarried couples are living with someone of a different faith according to Pew. About 18 percent of interfaith marriages, the largest percent, are between a Christian and someone who is unaffiliated.

Layla is originally from Burlington, Vermont, which is 86 percent white and 5 percent black. Less than 3 percent of people in Burlington identified as more than one race as of 2016.

"I find folks with liminal identities or dual identities have shared experiences of feeling distant from themselves and their families," she said. "I'm often assumed to be not Northern African or white enough, and the notions are absurd. I am what my blood is and what my cultures are."

Since the 2016 election, Layla has disconnected with members of her white family who she believes support Trump and his proposed Muslim ban. An article in *Al Jazeera* reported that Trump attempted to institute a Muslim ban in January 2017, which would forbid people from several predominantly Muslim countries from entering the US. including Iran, Iraq, Libya, Somalia, Sudan, Syria, and Yemen.

Layla identifies as Arab and "slightly Swedish." "I cope not by ever being 'white' because whiteness was defined to me as a pure racial group, unlike the others, from a young age," said Layla. "Whiteness is invented for the sake of exclusion amongst large ranges of ethnic groups." She added, "I've known since youth I'd never be white."

Like many in her situation, Layla has found that even her liberal, white family members can say and do things that make her uncomfortable as a person of color.

"I don't believe my older family members are socially capable, but I uphold relationships with the ones who try and have hope my family I've detached from will try to expand their hearts one day," said Layla. "They're like any other white family. I mean, my mother was in love with my father, but she is still socially white and can say things that are accidentally racist. She isn't overtly, or intentionally so."

Cirleen DeBlaere, who is Asian and white, was similarly influenced to go into her field because of her background. Cirleen is an associate professor in the counseling psychology program at Georgia State University, which is 25 percent white and 13 percent Asian. The highest population at the university is black, 42 percent.

Cirleen studies the psychological implications of race as it intersects with other identities, such as gender or sexuality, since "No identity develops in a vacuum."

"My racial and ethnic identity was generally treated separately from my gender," she said as an example. "As a society, I think we tend to define identity in very singular and isolated ways. This does not reflect reality. Everyone has multiple identities and they exist in tandem, are fluid, impact one another, and develop together. They are not isolated entities. We need to move away from these singular ways of thinking about identity and experience."

The lack of research into those with marginalized identities is a key component in why Cirleen became interested in her field. "These are narratives and experiences that have been historically overlooked in psychology," she said. "Marginalized identities on the whole have been underrepresented, but when we begin to consider multiple marginalized identities, their identities and experiences are even less centered and visible in the literature."

This idea has a name in psychology: "intersectional invisibility." Coined by Valerie Purdie-Vaughns, a black woman from Columbia University, and Richard P. Eibach, a white man from the University of Waterloo, intersectional invisibility is the idea that the more marginalized group a person is a part of, the less likely they are to be the focus.

For example, a white woman is more likely to be the focus of a study on women than a woman of color. Therefore, people's racial identities, whether mixed-race or monoracial, affect the perception of their gender, sexual orientation, etc., and vice versa.

In the study "Intersectional Invisibility: The Distinctive Advantages and Disadvantages of Multiple Subordinate-Group Identities," Valerie and Richard wrote that "disadvantage accrues with each of a person's subordinate-group identities," or that every identity a person has—a person can be a queer, Muslim woman, for example—impacts how a person is treated. Rather than acknowledging the above person as just Muslim, just a woman, or just queer, they are acknowledged as all three.

Cirleen believes that looking at marginalized identities that have been left out of the spotlight can actually lead to better understanding of all identities. "For example, we have a better sense of masculinity because we tried to understand the experiences of women better," she said. "Similarly, the idea of white and whiteness as a cultural identity is named and better understood because we name and understand marginalized identities."

As it pertains to mixed-race people and families, Cirleen's research focuses on how discrimination and prejudice affect the mental health of people of color. In meetings with patients, she promotes coping strategies for people of color among other oppressed groups.

"Of course, there can be challenges associated with having multiple ethnic identities," Cirleen said. "For example, multiracial people can experience a form of invalidation of their identities. Often, there is a complex relationship between a multiracial person's personal sense of identity and how others see them.

"We kind of joke that research is 'me'search," she added. "I think I was drawn to this area of research because of my own identity experience. As a biracial Asian American woman, my racial and ethnic identities and how I understand them has been a process."

She said that confusion is a common phenomenon among her multiracial patients, who are not seen as belonging to any specific group. "My first thought is that people think this way because this idea is explicitly and implicitly expressed to them. For example, for biracial Asian and white people, they are often not seen as white, but are also not accepted as fully Asian. I have heard this countless times from biracial Asian Americans.

"In fact, a lot of early literature on multiracial people tried to make the case that multiracial people would never be 'normal' or well-adjusted because they could never possibly fit in society or be fully accepted into any racial or ethnic group," she continued.

"This is false, of course, and also reflects the general racism and bias about people of different race and ethnicities having children."

She also emphasized that people who are not multiracial do not understand the concept of being more than one race, and thus reduce people who are multiracial to only one part of their identity. "Because multiracial people can be phenotypically ambiguous or look obviously multiracial, people tend to label, misidentify, or dictate to a multiracial person their identity," she said.

Even within families, Cirleen added, mixed-race people can experience racism. "A child may experience blatant racism from family members, but there can be a form of erasure that can also be very damaging," said Cirleen. By erasure, she said, "I mean that the multiracial identity and cultural group of the child may not be acknowledged and nurtured. This may be done explicitly or the child may receive the implicit message that talking about their identity is not okay."

This erasure can happen both with biracial children and with children adopted into families of a different race. "Children want to take care of their parents and tend to blame themselves," Cirleen said. "If there is any indication that not acknowledging one's identity would please the parents or family or make them more comfortable, children will try to accommodate this."

For white families who adopt young children of color, "I think the reasons behind an adoption or other circumstance can play a big role," said Cirleen. "If you are adopting because you exoticize children of other races or ethnicities, you are already beginning from a place of bias. If you are trying to 'rescue' a child, I think it is important to think about what you imagine you are rescuing the child from and what beliefs may be contributing to your thoughts about the child's circumstances. Being cognizant of racial issues and racism takes more than having a person of color in your family."

In 2000, the US became the first country to offer a mixed-race category as part of the census. It did so because the Census Bureau's Office of Management and Budget had seen a rise in the number of interracial marriages, according to their website. Over the next decade, the total US population increased by almost 10 percent, from 281,421,906 to 308,745,538, but the multiracial population increased by at least 50 percent, meaning multiracial people have become much more of a presence than they were ten years prior.

"When we live in a society that thinks of identity as singular and feels most comfortable when things are clearly defined, multiracial people pose an uncomfortable challenge that may make full acceptance by any single racial and ethnic group feel difficult," said Cirleen. "A lot of multiracial people talk about feeling more accepted by other multiracial people." Within families, "It takes recognizing that you benefit from the privilege that your family of color does not have and an ongoing and vigilant effort to combat racism.

"It has reinforced what so many before me have asserted," said Cirleen of her research. Over time, she has become more and more sure that "Race is a socially constructed thing. It is an artifact of hierarchy, privilege, and the maintenance of power. It is not a 'real' thing. We are not genetically different."

In fact, "There is more variability within different racial and ethnic groups than between them, yet we insist on its credibility,"

Cirleen added. "People of multiracial heritage challenge these understandings. I think that is at least one of the reasons that monoracism is perpetuated."

Interlude

José Moya teaches Latin American studies at Barnard College, which is 53 percent white and 12 percent Hispanic. He has written on immigration and is the author of the book *Cousins and Strangers: Spanish Immigrants in Buenos Aires.*

One would think that Latin American studies would have a lot to do with race, especially when looking at it from an institution in the US. For José, however, race is simply "a particularly imprecise and arbitrary concept for many reasons."

José himself is Cuban and Lebanese and was born in Cuba. In an interview for *The Daily Motion,* he said that he came to the US as a teenager and was immediately curious about the racial and ethnic diversity he saw in his new home.

"There are genetic differences between human groups that are important. For example, in making some of us more prone to certain illnesses than others," he said. "But these differences do not map out onto the racial categories and terms we use."

In terms of illnesses, it is true that certain genetic diseases are more often found in certain groups than in others. Tay-Sachs disease is most common among Ashkenazi Jews, who tend to be white. Other diseases, like diabetes and heart disease, are more common among black and brown people, but that is often because of environmental factors that stem from racism rather than genetic difference. For example, some research has found that stress from poverty and racism can increase a person's risk of heart disease.

Latin Americans in the US are difficult to classify using race. The US census offers several categories for race: white, black or African American, Asian, Native Hawaiian, other and two or more races. Often, Hispanic or Latinx people in the US have to check off "other" or pick another category, such as "black" or "white," unless they are multiracial.

In fact, the 2010 census went out of its way to define Hispanic and Latinx as an ethnicity rather than a race. "For this census," the form read, "Hispanic origins are not races." Instead, people filling out the form ticked "Hispanic, Latino or Spanish origin" in the category underneath.

The "Ancestry" category was also eliminated for the 2010 census. That meant that Arab Americans, for example, were classified as simply "white" along with European Americans, although they are treated very differently in practice. In 2020, the census will add a write-in section for the "white" and "black" categories. Examples on the 2018 census test for the white category include Egyptian, Italian, Lebanese, and others, while the black category lists African American, Jamaican, and Nigerian as examples.

"Where does Asia stop for Asian-Americans?" asked José. "In Israel, Iran, Turkey? Does it include the Asian part of Russia? Are white-skinned children of Algerians African-American and thus black? Latino or Hispanic is not legally a race but a multi-racial group, so in the census form we mark Hispanic and then in a different question choose among white, black, Asian, and so on. But in practice Latinos have been racialized. That is, turned into a race."

In his essay "Black and Blue and Blond," for example, author and editor Thomas Chatterton Williams noted that "for most of American history it was widely held that northern and southern Europeans constituted entirely separate races," commenting on how ideas of race have fluctuated for as long as the concept has been around.

"One would have to wonder why we keep on using a concept that is so meaningless," José continued. "But the reality is that these categories were never meant to be accurate, but to exclude some and preserve privilege for others. As long as the country was basically white and black, they were easier to maintain."

For a long time, race in the US was largely focused on the relationships between black and white US Americans. Immigrants with other identities, such as Clara Cardiello's parents and Nancy Generale's mother, have complicated the binary. Between 2000 and 2010, the US Hispanic population grew from nearly 13 percent to just over 16 percent, which means it grew from 50.8 to 57.5 million people in those ten years and accounts for about one-sixth of the US population. About one-third of Hispanics in the US are immigrants.

Other immigrant groups have also increased in the last few decades, since the 1965 Immigration and Nationality Act. Before that, national-origin quotas barred people from Asian and Arab countries from entering the US at all. Today, Asian immigrants to the US consist largely of those from China, India, Japan, the Koreas, the Philippines, and Vietnam, as reported by the Center for American Progress.

According to The Migration Policy Institute, there were 12 million Asian immigrants in the US in the year 2014. The majority of US American immigrants come from Latin America, followed by Asia. Asian immigrants are expected to overtake those from Latin American by the year 2055.

"Today, there are many minority groups who are much more educated and economically successful than whites," said José. "The proportion of Iranian-Americas or Indian-Americans or Taiwanese immigrants and their children who have a college education is twice as high as whites, and their average family income is like $20,000 higher."

According to the Migration Policy Institute, Asians are actually the most college educated immigrant group in the US, making up 46 percent of all college educated immigrants while white immigrants make up 28 percent. As for United States citizens, Asian Americans make $80,720 on average while white Americans make $61,349 according to data compiled by the US census.

Both immigration and the rising number of mixed-race marriages "Are changing the US and undermining the concept of race," said José. "In a sense, the US is becoming and will continue to become less parochial, more global."

José continued, "External physical traits like skin color will become less relevant in apportioning resources and status as other markers such as social class, education, manners, connections, etc., will become more important. It does not mean we will become an egalitarian society, but we are already becoming a more meritocratic one."

The fascinating thing about the US is the long history of racial tension that is different from other, more homogenous countries. From the beginning, the country was established by white people kicking natives out of their land and importing enslaved Africans.

"The US, because of its history of slavery, has had a greater obsession with race than most other countries," said José. "This does not mean that there is greater prejudice or 'racism' in the US. Actually one could argue that there is less inter-group violence in the US than in many other countries."

Journalist Miranda Larbi would agree that the US is not the only place with racial tensions. Miranda, a British reporter for *The Sun* and *MetroUK* in England, has an English mother and a Ghanaian father.

"I mean, it's a unique identity which comes with its own set of challenges," she said. "What are you, where are you from, are you X, Y, Z, are things that racially ambiguous people have to answer all the time. In the UK, having mixed raced kids has, in the past, had some rubbish connotations. I remember reading a long time ago about a woman who said she felt ashamed walking her kid in a pram because people would think she was lower class or a single parent if her kid was darker.

"Another thing is the obsession over having mixed race babies," she added. "Go on Instagram and there are accounts dedicated to swirl kids everywhere. They're such an exoticized commodity. I know loads of people who have said their dream would be to have a biracial kid, but isn't there an issue with that kind of racial planning? I don't know. It's just uncomfortable in my opinion."

Miranda has written extensively about being mixed-race in *MetroUK*, such as in her article "Having mixed race kids doesn't mean you're woke." In the article, which she published in October 2017, she spoke about how you can love someone of another race without being "woke" to, or aware of, racial issues: "I've dated plenty of white dudes who were perfectly nice and yet completely ignorant when it came to race. Blokes who laughed when their mates made racist jokes at my expense. Guys who talked about our relationship as a kind of exotic, erotic experiment. Men who asked me to straighten my hair because it made me look 'hotter.'"

Many experts cite the idea that race is interpreted differently in different countries as proof that race is a social construct, as Laura Generale believes. Thomas wrote in his aforementioned essay about his experience in France as someone who identifies as a "black man of mixed race heritage" that: "France long functioned as a haven for American black people ... precisely because, unlike in the US, we've been understood here first and foremost as American and not as black."

Of her articles, Miranda said that she "can be quite crude," but that she is not referring to "all white people because plenty of white folk are highly intelligent, my family included," she said. "Saying that, in arguments even my mum has said pretty weird things to my dad surrounding race which makes me think that, you know, even with very highly educated people, it's hard to erase all evidence of racial prejudice, even if they're married to someone of a different race and have kids."

Part Two

"Families don't have to match."–Leigh Anne Tuohy, guardian of football player Michael Oher

CHAPTER SIX

Finding the Balance

From the Pew Research Center: Nineteen percent of mixed-race adults in the US say their identity is an advantage, while 4 percent say it is a disadvantage, and 76 percent say it makes no difference.

AT 40 YEARS OLD, NINA WERBEL BLAUNER and her husband, Sid Blauner, were preparing for a baby. Unlike most expectant parents, however, they could not spend their days assembling cribs and baby-proofing their Riverdale apartment, since they did not know when, or even if, they would have a child, as often happens with the adoption process.

"Before we even met, something we separately both wanted to do was adopt a kid," said Nina of herself and Sid. "It was just something we both had strong feelings about. We both had a lot of love to share, and then it was hard for me to get pregnant, so we decided to go for it."

Instead of buying furniture they didn't know they would need, "We waited until the phone call arrived. It took a year from when we started the process, which is actually quick."

Now, Zeke, Nina's son, is 17. He attends St. Thomas More, a boarding school for boys in Oakdale, Connecticut. He plays basketball and is starting to think about applying to colleges. The biggest difference between Zeke and the rest of his family is that he does not look like them, since he is black and they are white.

"When you call the adoption agency, they ask you if you have any preferences, and we actually said we wanted to have a brown or black kid," Nina said. "We had found out in the interim— or maybe before that—that you can adopt a black kid very quickly, as opposed to a white kid, which could take years. And we also wanted to give love to someone who maybe couldn't get it as easily, so it was purposeful."

According to the National Public Radio's The Race Card Project, although about 15 percent of children in the US are black, black kids make up 24 percent of children in the US foster care system. It takes about 29 months for a black child in foster care to get adopted, whereas it takes 18 months for a white child.

It is also significantly less expensive to adopt a black child. It costs approximately $18,000 to adopt a black child and $35,000, nearly double, to adopt a white child. Articles by *ABC News* and *The Atlantic* have denounced the valuing of children by race within the adoption process, with *The Atlantic* likening the children to "salable commodities."

"I really feel, if you're going to share your love, that it should go to people who don't necessarily get chosen or picked or loved," she said. "I wanted to spread my love to a kid. There are plenty of people out there who have adopted white kids, and I didn't need to be that one."

Ethan, Nina's older son and Zeke's brother, was six when the adoption finally went through. "He had said he wanted a brown brother," said Nina of Ethan. "That was just his thing. We lived and he grew up in a building in Riverdale that was very much like how I grew up on the Upper West Side, where everybody is different. I could never be in a place where everyone looks the same."

At the time, "Ethan just had a lot of brown friends, and he was at a daycare where two gay fathers adopted a brown kid, and they were the only real people we knew who had adopted, so we spoke to them and they gave us the name of their agency."

Of Ethan and Zeke's relationship, Nina said, "It's great. It's always been great. Ethan has always been a great older brother, just very protective, and Zeke really enjoys being with Ethan. My sister and I were really close in age, and that was great, but it's also been really nice to have the bigger age difference. It allowed me to go through different things with them at different times in their life.

"Now, the relationship is also very good because now they can hang out as older kids hanging out," she continued. Since Ethan lives on the Lower East Side in Manhattan, "Zeke can go visit Ethan by himself in the city. They have a great relationship." At the same time, seeing Ethan and Zeke having to navigate the world so differently because of their skin color, "It breaks my heart."

What became difficult for Nina was walking the line between protecting her son emotionally and helping him navigate a world that treats kids of color differently from white kids. "It's hard, and it's always been hard," she said. "When he was little, I didn't want to tell him anything scary. I didn't want him to know that he would grow up in a world that treats him differently because of his skin. That's a sad thing. Now, I just think that he's older and he can handle things. We do talk about it more. You know, not to walk outside wearing a hood or what to do if he's stopped by police."

She continued, "I think as a parent, you talk to your kids about being safe in the world and not to do silly things, so it's not an unusual conversation. But it is a different conversation with him than I would have with my older son. It's easier now that he's older and I can be honest. He's not shielded. He understands what's happening in the world."

The adoption process is stressful for any parent. First, they have to hope they will be chosen at all. American Adoptions, an adoption agency that works with families, estimates that there are about 2 million couples waiting to adopt a child at any given time, or about 36 couples per one child who is to be adopted. It is even more difficult to adopt as a queer couple or single parent because of existing prejudices.

"She picks you, the birth mother," Nina said of her experience. "I put together a whole book and she picked us."

Then, the parents have to worry about the logistics, such as which state or country to adopt from. Nina and Sid chose Texas. Every state has their own laws regarding the rights of the birth parents and the adoptive parents and in Texas, Nina said, "The laws are really good in favor of the adopted parents."

She continued, "There's a year sort-of testing time, and then you have to go back to court. I didn't want to go, so Sid went. It turned out absolutely fine, but it's scary. You love this kid, and there's a chance you can't keep them."

Finally, "We got the call when she gave birth, or maybe the day before," said Nina about Zeke's birth mother. "We could have come that next day, but you have to get everything ready. And then a foster mom connected to the agency watches him for two weeks. But we got the phone call.

"His birth mom wanted to meet us, and that was a little weird," Nina added. "I didn't know what to say to her. It was very awkward for me. We didn't ask her a lot of questions, but I wish, in retrospect, we had asked more about the birth father. I was just so nervous to ask those questions."

With the whole family, "He's gotten tons of love," Nina said, smiling. "I think Sid was worried about his father accepting Zeke, but they couldn't have had a more beautiful relationship. From Sid's mom and my mom, I think he's gotten love all around. People like him. He's a likable kid. He's had a good life and the things that he's wanted to do, he's been able to do. He's incredibly talented, but humble about it. It's just part of him."

Going to pick up their son, Nina and Sid already felt that "There were going to be some issues, but more issues of the adoption itself," Nina said. "Whether Zeke was the same race as us or not, the adoption was a bigger issue than the race. I don't think I'd had a lot of thoughts about what would happen when he got older. I mean, because he's a teenager, he doesn't confide in me or anything, so I don't know, but I can imagine that there's a lot of things going on in his mind about it. I worry about that. The black and white thing I worry less about actually."

When Nina and Sid finally got to Texas, Zeke was two weeks old. "As soon as I held him in my arms, it was the same as holding Ethan in my arms," Nina said.

* * *

Nina is now 57 and working as a teacher for second graders in Bronxville. Even after 17 years of raising a black son as a white parent, she has not talked very much about race outside of her immediate family.

"I'm not sure that I have the answers," she said. "I always thought that race was a physical characteristic that people have, that you can see on the outside. I still feel that. It's a very dictionary definition, I guess. I mean, you can't always tell. It's a way of grouping people, and I think for the majority of people, you can see and group people by what they look like."

For Zeke, his race is prevalent everywhere he goes. "He just told me that, a few months ago, he was out with a bunch of friends and they walked into a store, and there was a police man there watching Zeke," said Nina. "All of the other kids were white, and he was watching Zeke."

Even traveling, Zeke is often targeted because he is black. On a recent trip to Israel, Zeke was held up by airport security because they did not believe he was Jewish, even though he was on a trip with other Jewish kids, all of whom were white.

"They ask you hundreds of questions to go through security, and everybody else went through, but they didn't believe him about why he was there," said Nina. "They had to call somebody over. They kept asking him what temple he was a part of and, since we were not part of any temple, he didn't know how to answer some of the questions. To be black is hard enough, but now he had to contend with being a black Jew."

Nina and Sid raised both of their sons to be Jewish. It is often difficult for Zeke to find diversity in Jewish spaces, although it has gotten easier over the years. Be'chol Lashon, an organization that works to strengthen the diversity of Jews globally and educating Jews about Jewish diversity, estimates that at least 20 percent of all Jews in the US are non-white or mixed-race.

"He's always played on a Jewish basketball team, Maccabiah," said Nina. "So he was the only black kid there. But last year or two years ago, when we went to Israel and Zeke represented the US, there were, like, five black kids on the team."

Of the diversity on the team, Nina said, "It was unbelievable and so great. A few were adopted. One was biracial. It was a cool thing for him. And in Israel it's great, because kids are all different colors." It's a change from the temple where Zeke went as a child, where "Zeke would be the only black kid."

On religion, "I'm actually an atheist, and the only reason we raised Ethan and Zeke Jewish is because of Sid's family," said Nina. "Zeke is actually around a lot of other religions now, so I'm not sure what he'll end up deciding, if he'll be religious or not. I think he'll make his own decisions. He's been with me enough and he knows how I feel about religion, and I really don't think his heart is in being Jewish, so I think he'll find his own path. Maybe he'll be religious and maybe he won't. But I don't think he was ever interested or passionate about it."

The family lived in several different places while Ethan and Zeke were growing up. First, Riverdale, where Nina and Sid lived when they adopted Zeke and which was 72 percent non-Hispanic white and about 8 percent black when the family lived there in the early 2000s, though Nina said her building was much more diverse.

The family moved to Mount Vernon, which is 61 percent black and 19 percent white. There, Ethan and Zeke attended the

Bronxville school where Nina worked. Bronxville is 88 percent white and less than 1 percent black.

"The kids were allowed to go there, so Ethan started at Bronxville in sixth grade, and then all his friends were there. I was driving back and forth, and that got to be a pain, so we decided to move closer, mostly for Ethan.

"Bronxville was just so white. I mean, Ethan graduated from there, and Zeke had a great experience. He started in first grade. The reason he was accepted was because he was a phenomenal athlete and the school was all about athletics. Had he not had that, I probably wouldn't have sent him there. We had to think about that. But he's such a friendly kid that he just meets people everywhere. And at that age, I don't think kids are really looking at skin color. He was there in middle school, and he liked it.

Nina said she knew only one other black student at Bronxville in Zeke's year. Eventually, the family moved because "We wanted to give Zeke the opportunity to date and have friends the same race as him." Since then, "He's dated white girls and he's dated black girls. I mean, I'm not sure if he would have dated white girls had he not been raised or gone to school in predominantly white environments. But he met them on his own."

Now, Zeke goes to St. Thomas More in Oakdale, in the town of Montville, which is 86 percent white and 5 percent black, though Nina said Zeke's school is more diverse. "When I went up this last time, there were tons of black kids, which I was thrilled about. I had no idea, but now I think it's pretty diverse. Although there are no girls, so that's a bummer," she joked. At St. Thomas More, all students of color make up approximately 39 percent of the student body. For the average boarding school in the US, that number is 21 percent.

Recently Zeke has started asking more questions about his biological mother and saying that he may want to meet her. "Last year, he started to, and we got all the paperwork," Nina said. "You have to be 18 to do it without all the paperwork, but I thought we'd get it together. The agency no longer exists, so it will take a bit of effort, but it will be worth it if that is what Zeke decides."

One study on adolescent American adoptees found that Zeke is in the majority concerning his biological parents: 65 percent of subjects wanted to meet their birth parents according to the study, which was done by the American Adoption Congress.

"Zeke's birth mother was 17, and she wanted to attend college and play basketball," Nina said. "Because of this, she felt she couldn't raise a child at that time in her life."

Of Zeke's desire to find his birth mother, "He talks about it sometimes, and then will just kind of drop it, but I think he'll do it," Nina said. "I'll help him do it, to find her, because I think it's hard and a little scary, too. I don't know if we'll find her, and then, if we find her, if she'd want to see him, which would be just a horrible, horrible thing. In general, Zeke is a happy kid, but I'm sure there are parts about being adopted that are always hard."

On reflecting, Nina thinks that Zeke has "100 percent had advantages that he couldn't have had" with his birth parents. "He's traveled and gone to camps," she said. "We're not a wealthy family, but he's been given incredible opportunities that he never would have had. Besides just his lifestyle, I think it will help when he applies to schools. Schools want interesting families, so I think he'll have an advantage there."

Through Zeke, Nina said, her world view has entirely evolved. "It opens you up," she said of loving someone so different from her in terms of race. "It's opened my eyes to small things, such as his curly hair, to big things, like race. I am much more cognizant of how race plays such a big role in our lives.

"Just paying more attention to the world around me and caring more about the world around me," she added. "It's a tough place. It's also opened my eyes as a teacher to be mindful of people with differences, no matter what those differences are."

Although Nina said she does not often have to explain her family structure to most people, Zeke has made her rethink how she talks to her students about families. "Because I teach seven and eight-year-olds, they'll say anything. That's who kids are. When they see something that looks different, they'll blurt it out. This year, I have two mothers that have kids in the class. That's huge in Bronxville. I have a divorced family, and there are hardly any."

Recently, she spoke to her kids about Zeke "with that idea in mind, that I didn't want any kid to feel that, because their family is different, that that's a bad thing or a negative thing. But besides seven- and eight-year-olds, I've never felt the need to explain us or wanted to. It's never even crossed my mind, really.

"I have a huge poster in my class that says 'Be a fruit loop in a world full of Cheerios,'" she added. "That's just such an important part of who I am and who I want my kids to be. It's a great thing to be different and to be comfortable in your own skin, no matter what. I feel like he's taught that to me. I think I'd still feel this way, but I'm even more passionate about it."

CHAPTER SEVEN

Enough

From the American Psychological Association: Many US schools only allow students to check off one race on registration and other forms.

EVEN SOMETHING AS SMALL AS walking through a drug store can remind Gillian Sherman, who is Chinese, that she is different from the rest of her family, all of whom are white. The "flesh color" band-aids, she said, do not match her skin like they would match her blond-haired, blue-eyed brother Andrew's. In one instance, she ran into another Asian woman in a CVS in the same aisle, and the two commiserated together.

"She looked over and we had a brief conversation about how the 'flesh color' band-aids were clearly designed for Caucasians, and did not include people whose skin color was not fair," Gillian said.

Gillian, 20, was adopted as a baby by her father, Eric Sherman, and mother, Heidi Beutler. The couple already had a son when they decided to adopt, Andrew Sherman, who is their biological child and who is three years older than Gillian. Gillian is the only person of color in her family, immediate or extended.

For the most part, Gillian's friends at school are white. She is a junior at Guilford College, which is 57 percent white and nearly 5 percent Asian. Gillian does, however, have several close Asian friends and friends of other races. Greensboro, where Gillian went for college in 2015, is 45 percent non-Hispanic white and 4 percent Asian, largely Vietnamese and Indian.

"I think that people my age who are Chinese, or even Asian, I am able to connect with them more," she said. More important, though, is that people are her age or going through similar experiences. "People who are older, I do not necessarily have a stronger connection just because they're Asian," she said. "In my experience, the generational gap is something that has been a pretty significant barrier in regards to sharing experience."

Growing up, Gillian did not always fit in with her Asian peers, since her family was white. Sometimes, she was referred to as an 'Oreo,' but more often that was used to refer to a black person raised in a white family. "I have actually been called a 'fortune cookie' before." In her opinion, this "does not make a lot of sense since fortune cookies are an American invention, but the intent is still there," she said.

Among her black and Latinx peers, especially those who were raised by black or Latinx parents, Gillian does not always know how to react to racism or discrimination. Although it stings to be called a 'fortune cookie' or to never see people who look like her on screens—*Crazy Rich Asians*, made in 2018, was the first movie with an all Asian cast since *The Joy Luck Club* in 1993—she wonders if she really has it so bad.

"I am not part of a more discriminated group, and that does play a strong factor to my experience as a person of color," she said. "At times I ask myself, 'Do I get to feel discriminated against? Do I really deserve to feel like this?' Sometimes I feel guilty because I do feel like the target of discrimination, but the discrimination I experience is nowhere near as intense as other minority groups feel."

In time, Gillian said, she has realized that "discrimination is discrimination no matter who you are, what the experience is, or what the impact is. Whatever you feel in response to discrimination is valid and deserves compassion."

Although she does not look like her family, she does have an American name, since her family changed her Chinese name, Rao Li Lin, to Gillian upon adopting her. She does not know Mandarin or Cantonese.

"Especially as a kid, and even as I grow older, I struggle to identify with an identity group," she said. "My appearance shows that I am absolutely Asian, but I have an American name and I can't speak a word of Chinese."

She added, "Not being able to feel like I could 100 percent identify as white or Chinese caused a bit of an identity crisis for me when I hit 13 and ended up having a negative impact of my self-image and self-esteem. Not being able to feel like you can fully identify yourself, it can create a serious and damaging issue that I don't think a lot of people consider when adopting a child from another country."

* * *

When Gillian heard that Donald Trump had been elected president of the US, she was at Guilford in Greensboro. Later, she would find that the election would have repercussions among her family back in Manhattan, as well. Manhattan, where Gillian and her family are from, is 48 percent non-Hispanic white and 12 percent Asian as of 2012.

"I think the biggest difference that I noticed was with my family members who are older," she said. "My mom, dad, aunts, and uncles. I'm only 20, so my viewpoint on issues like religion and politics are simply different, but I think even more so actually because I am a different race than my family. I think my family is aware of racial issues, but not necessarily more than any other family."

She continued, "I have noticed in the past year and a half that my family does not, and will not ever, know what it is like to experience America as a person who is of a minority group. When I talk to my family about societal or political issues, there is a lack of understanding on both sides, as I will never fully understand their perspective and they will never understand mine. My family is incredibly lucky and privileged and I think that they unintentionally take that for granted."

Growing up, Gillian said, race was actually "something that we inevitably talked about pretty often. I think the fact that I had different skin and different hair than my mom and brother, it became something that was always on my mind and was not something that was ever considered taboo or uncomfortable to talk about."

To not talk about it would have been strange, since "I do stick out in family photos because my skin color is slightly more tan and my hair is darker in comparison to my family's pale skin and bleach-blond hair."

Just like psychologist Cirleen DeBlaere's research showed, Gillian said her physical appearance and her ethnic background makes her feel distant from her white family. Gillian described it as "not being able to fully identify."

"I believe that part of my identity crisis, which still hasn't really ended, has to do with the fact that I will never be 'enough' of one culture or belong 'enough' to one country," she said. "I was born in China, but I can't speak Chinese. I've lived in America for 20 years, so to people in China, I am not 'Chinese enough.' To Americans, I will never be 'American enough' because I was born in China and I don't look 'American.'"

She continued, "There is this really fine line of which country and culture you belong to. I definitely believe that people who are biracial or bicultural can understand, or at least relate to, this feeling like you don't belong to just one."

Even if she hadn't grown up talking about race with her family, Gillian is sure that her thoughts and opinions have been influenced by her race, especially "in regards to issues like socioeconomic class and other political issues.

"It wasn't until about middle and high school that I got old enough to realize that my thoughts and opinions would be different not because I disagreed with my family, but because I was experiencing America through different eyes than they were," she added.

As she has gotten older, "Our conversations about race have naturally become more complex and dynamic," Gillian said. "But in the past year and a half, I would say that there is a clear difference in opinion. They're not negative or offensive by any means, but they can never fully understand the situations and feelings I have regarding race because they do not know what it is like to experience America through the eyes of someone who is not white.

"No matter how much we may want to deny it, you can never fully understand or judge a perspective unless you experience it yourself," she continued. "In the past year and a half, my different opinions between my family and me have become even more noticeable and obvious, but I do feel like it has caused my family and me to become even more patient with each other and feel a deeper level of understanding and compassion."

CHAPTER EIGHT

Jujubes Represent Sugar

From the American Psychological Association: Multiracial adolescents are not as subject to stereotype threat as other minorities.

JAE LANGTON, LIKE MOST 13-YEAR-OLD BOYS, loves to antagonize his mother. Shelley Langton sighed as her son attempted to tie his socks around his feet and asked, "Can you put them on normal, please?" Jae put his socks on, rolling his eyes as he did. The Langtons's brown mutt, Schuyler, took a swipe at one of them.

Also like most teenage boys, Jae does not pay much attention to politics. At one point, he said, "All I know is Kim Jong-un," referring to the Supreme Leader of North Korea. Jae dressed up as Kim Jong-un once for Halloween.

Even though he is Korean—he was born just outside of Seoul—Jae does not feel like Trump's policies will hurt him in any way. "I'm okay during Donald Trump's presidency because of the fact that I'm from a white family and it doesn't really affect me that much," he said.

Jae was adopted from South Korea as a baby in 2004 by Shelley and her husband, David, who are both white. According to the Center for Disease Control, Jae is one of more than 250,000 children who have come to the United States from another country through international adoption between 2002 and 2017.

When they decided to adopt, Shelley and David already had a biological daughter, Rachael, who is nine years older than Jae. From the time Shelley and David started the adoption process to the time they got Jae took two years, twice as long as it took Nina Werbel Blauner to adopt Zeke.

"You can see their picture up on the bookcase," Shelley said, pointing to a large photograph of Rachael, blond and blue-eyed, holding black-haired Jae.

"That's the picture from when he came," Rachael said. "That was in the airport. I was really excited, because I wanted to be an older sister really badly, so that was really cool."

Shelley, Rachael, and Jae sat in the living room together on a Sunday afternoon. Rachael and Shelley conversed. Jae played with his phone, since his socks were no longer an option.

"I have adopted siblings, a sister and brother who are Korean," said Shelley. "When David and I got married, we talked about if we would ever adopt, and I said if we did choose to adopt, I would definitely want to adopt from Korea because I have Korean people in my family. So it was very specific."

Shelley grew up in Minnesota, where there is a large percentage of Korean adoptees in the US. According to Eleana Kim's 2011 book *Adopted Territory: Transnational Korean Adoptees and the Politics of Belonging*, other states with large populations of Korean adoptees include Idaho, Massachusetts, Montana, New York, Oregon, and Vermont.

"I actually asked if we could adopt through the same agency in Minnesota where my parents adopted from because they offer this amazing support service, but they didn't support homes in New York," said Shelley. "So, they recommended the place where we did end up adopting Jae through, so I said, well, one of the things I was really concerned about and wanted to make sure we had access to was post-adoption supports, not just the getting ready."

The Langtons live in Ardsley, New York, near Jenna Lowry and her parents. Jae recently graduated from Ardsley Middle School and will attend Ardsley High School next, where Rachael graduated from in 2013. After Ardsley High School Rachael went to Ithaca College, which is about 72 percent white and nearly 4 percent Asian.

"Ardsley is more of a diverse one than other schools, than other towns," Jae said.

"Do you have any other friends that are Korean?" Shelley asked Jae.

Jae shook his head. "No."

"Is there anyone else in your grade who's Korean?"

"Oh, yes," he said. He mentioned one other student, a boy in his school named Will.

"Most of your friends are white, though," said Shelley.

Jae nodded. "Yes," he said.

Jae knows one person of color that he considers to be a friend, a boy named Aaron who is Turkish, and Shelley said there are several families on their block that are Chinese or Indian. Other than that, Jae said that most of his friends at school are white.

"But you don't think about it that way, that they're white and you're Asian," said Shelley.

"No," said Jae.

"Before we got Jae, I thought about that," Shelley said. "I mean, we had gotten through the system as far as third grade with Rachael, so we were familiar with a little bit of the diversity of the schools, and I thought it was mostly, I would say, Indian and Asian, maybe Chinese people."

According to Shelley, the few Korean people from Ardsley that she did know were very interested when she told them she was about to adopt Jae. When she told the Korean women she knew from the local nail salon that she was going to adopt from South Korea, Shelley said they had a lot of advice.

"They had very mixed feelings in the beginning," she said.

Rachael nodded. "They want to make sure that you're raising him right," she said.

"I mean, it must be strange to be from a culture and seeing a white family raising a kid from that culture," said Shelley. "We used to have a neighbor across the street who was Korean, and they would invite Jae to come over and play. I think there was a little bit of a sense of 'He needs to know what his heritage is.'" Often, Shelley said, Jae would come home talking about how he didn't like the Korean food his friend's family served.

Today, the rules about adopting from South Korea are even stricter than when Shelley and David adopted Jae. Only couples are allowed to adopt and they have to have been married for at least three years. Couples must be between 25 and 44 years old according to Spence-Chapin, an adoption organization.

New Beginnings, an international adoption agency, notes that couples can be as old as 49 as long as one parent is part Korean, at least one parent is a Korean adoptee, or the parents have previously adopted from Korea. Both parents must have a body mass index below 30 percent and must not have any health problems.

More generally, adoption laws change often. For example, it was not until March 31, 2016, that a federal judge overturned a Mississippi ban on same-sex couples adopting children, making it legal in every state.

At home, even though Shelley and David think it is very important for Jae to know where he came from, they don't think of him as adopted or Asian.

"I think of him as my son," said Shelley. "And I guess I think of him as like me. When Trump became president, I think the focus in our family has been more about women and how he treats women. There definitely was a thought about, 'How is this going to affect people of color?' and 'Is this going to affect Jae? Is he going to be targeted in any way?' But I think a lot of it is the community that we live in. It's very progressive, very tolerant."

Shelley and David wanted Jae to have a connection with his Korean culture, even in America. Every year since he was five, Jae has participated in Camp Friendship, an organization with a week-long program for Korean children. In the summer of 2018, Jae went back as a counselor.

"There are a lot of Chinese camps," said Shelley. "I think because the adopted Chinese population is so big." Where Shelley grew up, however, there was a camp for Korean adoptees called Camp Kiwi. "My brother and sister went there, so we said when we adopted that we would definitely want to keep the culture." Of Camp Friendship, Shelley said, "This is like the only place Jae can go and be with all Korean kids who are adopted. It's a community of all people like him."

Shelley also met several other people who have Korean children who are adopted through Camp Friendship and through a playgroup Jae went to when he was younger, a group of adopted Korean boys.

"His first birthday, we did a whole Korean-themed birthday," Rachael said. "We had some Korean tradition where the baby has ten items in front of him and the first one he chooses shows something about his future. He chose jujubes."

"What do jujubes represent?" Shelley asked. "Sweetness?"

"I don't remember," Rachael admitted.

"Hell if I know," said Jae.

Rachael smiled. "He chose them because sugar," she said.

* * *

By the time David came home from church, Jae had already gone upstairs to enjoy his Sunday in peace. David joined Shelley and Rachael in the living room, where we were discussing Jae's biological parents.

"We have the names," David said, taking Jae's seat. "Not a lot of details."

"We know they were tall," Rachael said.

"Yeah, we have their education, their heights," said Shelley. After Jae grew several inches this year, Shelley and David checked the records they got when they adopted Jae, wondering about his biological parents. "We have a paragraph of information on the family," Shelley added. "His biological father is five foot ten. It was very tall for a Korean."

Jae has not spent long periods of time in South Korea, but the whole family agrees that they would all like to go back to South Korea for a while, just not to meet Jae's birth parents. According to Rachael, Jae has said he would not want to meet them—"not right now," said Rachael—although he would be interested in meeting his foster parents from South Korea.

"A couple people he knows have met their foster families and they have a connection," said Shelley. "The foster families, this tends to be a job for them, taking care of these babies. Many of them seem to still have fond memories."

"They had pictures of him," Rachael added. "In Korea, you celebrate your 100th day, and they had a huge party for him with all these pictures."

"At one point, he said he never wanted to meet his biological father," said Shelley. "He's very angry. I don't know why. We never talk about it, except the basics of why a family would give a child up for adoption. We never talked about anything about what might have happened with his biological family. We do know that the mother was college educated and the father was not, so maybe it was something about that, that the parents said, 'You can't marry someone who isn't college educated.' But there was a while where he was really angry."

"When he was three, when he got mad at my mom, he would say that she was his third favorite mom," Rachael said.

"Yeah, well he would say, 'I wish I hadn't come here.'"

Rachael laughed. "No, no, he would say, 'You're my third favorite mom.'"

"Well, one time, he said, 'Well, why did I have to come here. I had two other moms,'" said Shelley. "So, one time later, he said, 'Mom, I love you.' And I said, 'Thank you, that's such a compliment because I know you have two other moms,' just to tease him a little bit." Everyone laughed.

According to David, the international adoption process "was actually more appealing because of the way the children are in foster care and are brought to us as opposed to the whole process of American adoption, where you almost have to advertise to find someone who's willing to give up a baby. It was a process that just didn't feel right. So this was much more, here's a baby that's in need and here's a way we can fulfill this need."

"Actually, that reminds me that one of the risks of adopting locally, domestically, is that we were told mothers here have more rights," Shelley added. "So they can take the baby away up to a much longer time, whereas with international adoptions—probably because there's less rights for women, but also because it's international—it's actually safer, or more secure. That definitely played into our decision as well."

In her essay "Big Night," author Jill Sisson Quinn writes that, when she was preparing to adopt, the initial fees were around

$3,000. However, if the birth mother changed her mind during pregnancy or within thirty days after the birth, Quinn and her husband would end up paying around $5,000. Quinn says the adoption agency called this a "false start."

In addition to Shelley's brother and sister, David also has cousins who are adopted, though they are white. And just like David's children, his cousins are also a mix of adopted and biological children. "My mom's only got one brother, and he has a biological son and two adopted daughters," he said.

"That's interesting because my friends are always so fascinated by the fact that we're one biological, one adopted, and I never thought of that as being a weird thing before," said Rachael. "But my friend does that all the time, where she says, 'I don't know how that dynamic would work.'"

Several websites claim that many families have both biological and adopted children, including America's Adoption Agency, like with Ethan and Zeke Blauner and Andrew and Gillian Sherman. The Center for Disease Control notes that about 1 percent of women in the US ages 18 to 44 adopted in 2016, and about half of those women already had a biological child.

"Well, I think the age gap is bigger than the difference of adopted versus not adopted," said David.

"And when we talk to the kids, you know, kids are different," said Shelley. "Rachael and Jae are different. There's similarities and there's differences. And sometimes, when I'm frustrated by the differences, and I talk to families that have all biological kids, they say, 'Listen, you can have two biological kids who are very different from each other. It's not just because one's adopted and one's biological.'"

According to Shelley and David, Rachel is more like David, and Jae is more like Shelley. For example, Shelley and Jae both have a great sense of direction. Rachael and David do not.

"It's funny because me and my dad have more similar personalities, so there's that crossover," Rachael said. "Jae and I were having a conversation once about which parent are you, and Jae was like, 'Mom and I just have that special connection.'" The whole family, however, loves musicals.

"We were in the car driving down the road last summer and singing *Hamilton* at the top of our lungs, Jae included," said Shelley.

"And we were like, okay, I guess this isn't really in the genes," said David. "He says it's just *Hamilton*, but I've noticed it in other things, not just in musicals. I used to think all these things Rachael did were biological because, well, you know, it's in the genes. She has to love musicals and she has to do stuff that's just part of being in this family because it's in the genes. And then I see Jae do them. And I'm like, uh-oh, this is a learned thing."

CHAPTER NINE

From Noah to Elias, Leah, and Rebekkah

From the US Census Bureau: The population of multiracial people who are black and white grew the most between 2000 and 2010.

APPROXIMATELY 40 PERCENT OF ADOPTIONS in the US are transracial, meaning a family of one race adopting a child of another, based on America Adopts statistics from 2016. Most of these adoptions came from China, according to the US State Department.

More recently, rates of interracial adoption are falling. In 2005, 585 children were adopted into families that identified as a different race than they did in the US, the most interracial adoptions of any year on record. In 2011, there were only 288 interracial adoptions.

As interracial adoption rates fall, so do rates of international adoption, according to the US State Department in 2018. Additionally, The Intercept reported that, "Country after country has suspended or shrunk its adoption program, leaving a greatly reduced supply to meet a US demand for adoptable children that hasn't waned." They estimate that international adoptions shrunk by approximately 80 percent in the 14 years between 2004 and 2018.

World-wide, 22,989 children were adopted in 2004, while 4,714 were adopted by the end of 2017. Several adoption agencies actually went out of business in that time.

The history of interracial adoption is actually quite short. In 1944, the Boys and Girls Aid Society began a campaign called "Operation Brown Baby," meant to increase the number of children of color placed into homes, as there were fewer families of color adopting at the time. The campaign took off in 1947, after a white family adopted a Chinese baby, Noah Turner.

Criticism of interracial adoption comes from all sides. Many say interracial adoption can cause low self-esteem for children because they are not being raised to understand their history. Many studies, such as one conducted by the International Journal for the Advancement of Counseling called "Transracial Adoption of Koreans: A Preliminary Study of Adjustment," negate those criticisms, suggesting it is up to the parents to raise their children with an understanding of their culture.

These studies are true for children of all races. The most important thing, researchers at the *Journal of Family Psychology* found, is for the parents to acknowledge differences and encourage cultural understanding.

Shari Goldstein is the owner of Carolina Mornings Asheville Vacation Rentals in Asheville, North Carolina, and the mother of two daughters. Rebekkah Whetten-Goldstein, now Rebekkah Skarohlid, was 17 months old when she was adopted, while younger daughter Leah Whetten-Goldstein was five months old. Goldstein adopted both girls from China with her partner at the time, Kate Whetten. Both Shari and Kate are white.

"From the day we adopted Bekkah, we celebrated diversity and being adopted with the girls," Shari said. "I would always buy books about different families, whether they looked the same or different from our family, with different cultural and ethnic backgrounds or families that only had one mom or two dads. We had to special order a lot of these books from publishers, but it was always something I embraced."

At the time she adopted her daughters, Shari said, "We lived in a very Caucasian community, without much diversity in families, so I really tried to have a lot of those resources around."

In addition to books about adoption and Chinese culture, Goldstein's daughters also watched cartoons with Asian characters, such as the Disney movie *Mulan* and the Miyazaki film *My Neighbor Totoro*. They attended Chinese school as well as Chinese language lessons.

In the same 14 years that international adoptions decreased by nearly 80 percent, adoptions from China were no exception. While 7,038 babies were adopted from China in 2004, 1,905 were adopted from China by the end of 2017, a 73 percent decrease.

Shari and Kate adopted their daughters in 1994 and 1995. In April 1992, before Shari and Kate adopted their older daughter,

China had implemented a law allowing international adoptions, according to research by Brandeis University.

"Well, we knew that we wanted to adopt because using a sperm donor could become very expensive and was never a guaranteed success, and then we were thinking about what would be the best way to adopt," said Goldstein. "Adopting in the states, adopting a white baby, was even more expensive and it took a long time.

"My father loved China and all things Chinese, and Kate was an Asian history major in undergrad, so we both had background in Chinese history," Shari continued. "China seemed like a culture that we both embraced earlier." Plus, she said, "Having a family was number one."

Part of Shari's efforts to encourage her daughters to explore their racial identity included introducing them to other Chinese adoptees.

"We started Camp China, where adopted families with children from China get together every summer and celebrate Chinese culture," said Shari. "So we started that in North Carolina and it's still going on now."

Shari and Kate, with the help of friends Nelda Bradley and Debbie Lucas, founded Camp China in 1999, when their daughters were seven and four. Activities include Chinese dance, making dumplings and celebrating holidays such as the Chinese New Year, the moon festival and the lantern festival. There are family programs as well as programs for the children.

The family's experience at Camp China led to a trip they look in 2002 through an organization called Adoption Family Travel.

"They organize trips for adopted families to go to the child's birth country and discover their heritage," Shari said. "This trip was the start of my daughters' traveling to China." With Shari's younger daughter especially, "She loves China and loves going there," Shari said. "She really wants to be around other Asians."

There are several programs across the country that provide spaces for adopted children, such as Jae Langton's Camp Friendship, which was founded in 1984 for Korean adoptees. They expanded to include a program for Chinese adoptees in 2008.

Shari said her experiences have led her to be more open to talking about race. "People will ask me, 'Who's your daughter?' and I'll say 'The Asian one,'" she said. "The other day I was meeting someone for coffee, an accountant, and he said, just so I knew who he was, that he was wearing a checkered shirt, and I said, 'I am Caucasian and I'll be wearing a black shirt.' I like to do that so people are aware. It's okay to say what color we are. It's something to be proud of and embrace."

Now, Rebekkah lives in Chapel Hill, North Carolina, which is 73 percent white and 12 percent Asian, and Leah is studying law in San Francisco, California, which is 48 percent white and 33 percent Asian.

"The school I chose has a lot of professors who are women of color," said Leah about the University of San Francisco's law program. "I think it's important, as someone who's not white going into a very white dominated field, to have mentors specifically for how you survive and cope with that. And great mentors are people who have done that themselves."

Of course, everyone's experiences are different. Elias Smolcic-Larson, a student at Guilford College in Greensboro,

North Carolina, where Gillian Sherman is also a student, said he has had a hard time understanding his role in a white family. Elias was adopted from Ecuador.

"Especially when I'm interacting with my Trump supporting family, it has been hard and we have had some very uncomfortable situations with their coworkers asking ignorant questions and giving some rather unpleasant looks," said Elias.

"It is especially evident when I interact with other Latinx people who often perceive me as not one with my family," he continued. "In a way, my father is more understanding and accepting of these differences. My mother wants me to identify more with her and her culture, but it is becoming increasingly hard to do that."

Alternatively, he notes that his Hispanic friends will often say he is very white because of the way he was raised.

"I usually respond with speaking with Spanish or doing something very Hispanic," he said. "I have also been asked by adults if I identify as white and I say, I am, for sure, culturally, but not ethnically, and I am slowly trying to adopt a fusion of cultures."

Interlude

SINCE 1962, *A WRINKLE IN TIME*'S Meg Murray has always been white. That all changed on March 9, 2018, when the new film adaptation hit theaters. The movie stars the biracial actress Storm Reid as Meg, Gugu Mbatha-Raw as her mother, and Chris Pine as her father. Gugu is black and white while Chris is white. In the film, Meg's younger brother Charles Wallace Murray is adopted and played by Filipino actor Deric McCabe. There is no mention of race in the movie.

By the time the film premiered, while mixed-race families were not entirely the norm, they were far more commonplace than they had been even a few years before. For example, in September 2014, more than 11 million viewers watched as Rainbow Johnson, played by biracial actress Tracee Ellis Ross, challenged her husband Andre's notion of what it means to be black on the series premiere of the ABC sitcom *Black-ish*.

Now in its fourth season, *Black-ish* has spawned a spin-off, *Grown-ish*, starring Yara Shahidi, who plays Rainbow and Andre

Johnson's daughter on the show and whose parents are African American and Iranian American. It is one of many television shows to include biracial families, including *Modern Family* and *Jane the Virgin*. The Emmy award-winning *Black Mirror* episode "San Junipero," also starring Gugu, prominently features a mixed-race couple played by Gugu and Canadian actress Mackenzie Davis.

Many movies have also depicted interracial couples in recent years, such as *The Big Sick* (2017), written by Emily V. Gordon, who is a white American, and Kumail Nanjiani, who is Pakistani. The screenplay is based on their real-life relationship. This is the film that Joy Sheenan said reminds her of her grandparents' relationship.

Other films that depict mixed-race relationships include *Everything, Everything* (2017), which stars biracial actress Amandla Stenberg as Madeline Whittier and white actor Nick Robinson as Olly Bright; *The Greatest Showman* (2017) which stars biracial actress Zendaya as Anne Wheeler and white actor Zac Efron as Phillip Carlyle; and *The Hate U Give* (2018), also starring Amandla as Starr Carter and New Zealander K.J. Apa as her boyfriend, Chris, although Amandla's character is explicitly not biracial in this film.

The history of interracial couples in the media started long before the movies and TV shows listed above, the earliest of which premiered in 2009. Many early films depicted interracial relationships between a powerful white man and a reluctant native woman, such as *The Bronze Bride*, which premiered in 1917. In 1951, *I Love Lucy* became the first television show to depict a married interracial couple when white actress Lucille Ball insisted that Cuban actor Desi Arnaz, her real-life husband, portray her husband on television.

The first interracial kiss on television occurred in 1968 between black actress Nichelle Nichols and white actor William Shatner when their characters were forced together by aliens on *Star Trek. The Jeffersons*, which premiered in 1975, featured an interracial couple, the Jefferson's neighbors, and their biracial daughter.

According to Trey Ellis, a professor of media studies at Columbia University, in recent years there has been an increase in diversity in all media. Trey teaches screen writing and creative writing. He is an African American man who is married to an Italian American woman and has two biological African American children from his first marriage, a white and Asian stepdaughter from his wife's first marriage, and an adopted black child.

Trey said it is important to show students examples of casting from stereotypes in addition to real life so that they can learn to do the opposite. He used police officers as an example: "At first, they might think 'cop,' he's going to eat donuts and he's going to be Irish and he's going to be big," he said.

"And then, I say look out the window," Ellis continued. "What does the policeman in New York City look like? It might be a Dominican woman who's heavyset and about five-foot tall. It might be a Sikh man who's six-foot-three with a turban, right? So, any of those things you add to your story, they make your story much richer."

In his view, such an understanding of diversity in real life can benefit screenwriters in making their films stand out. "Suddenly, you treat people like they're real, because you've actually done casting from real life instead of from central casting," he said.

Trey noted that as early as the 1950s, when African American and multiracial characters were barely visible in movies and television shows, advertisers, intent on reaching their full potential audience, used black actors in commercials.

"In the 1950s, even, there had been commercials with black people in them," said Trey. "Advertisers use data, while Hollywood would just sort of use their feeling, so there was really a big lag." As a result, black actors were limited to stereotypical roles in movies such as "the black best friend" and other "hyper-positive" roles. "And in police procedurals, the chief of police or some sort of supervisor," Trey added. "Gruff, old black guy. Certainly, judges."

More recently, the miscasting of characters of color as white actors has come to light. Often, it is Asian characters that get erased, such as in *Aloha*, which premiered in 2015 and which cast white actress Emma Stone as a multiracial white, Chinese, and Hawaiian woman. *Ghost in the Shell*, a 2017 movie based on a Japanese anime starring white actress Scarlett Johansen, is another example. "It's my favorite story, just because it's just the most egregious," said Trey of what he called "the whitewashing of Asians in cinema."

In the past, he said, it was difficult for mixed-race people to identify with anyone they saw on television because mixed-race actors often pretended they were one race, and for simplicity's sake, parents in family shows were usually cast as the same race. Mixed-race actors, he said, were often pressured to identify with one race over another.

In the age of social media, it is much easier today for those in the spotlight to talk about their mixed-race identity, as well, whereas decades ago, they had much less control over their own narrative. Tracee, Yara, and others have spoken openly about their mixed-race ancestry online.

Although there are still issues in casting mixed-race actors, such as with *Aloha*, there has been more of a push to include multiracial actors in recent years. This is true even when the storyline is not about race. Additionally, paying attention to advertisements today, Trey said he has seen more and more families that look like his own. That is, multiracial.

As racial diversity increases within families in film, so do the types of families we see on TV. *Modern Family*, which premiered in 2009, features gay, white fathers who adopt an Asian daughter. One couple consists of a Colombian woman with one biological Colombian child and a white man with two biological white children. In the show's fourth season, the latter couple has a Colombian and white child together.

Another example is *Jane the Virgin*, which premiered in 2014. In it, Jane Gloriana Villanueva, a Venezuelan and Mexican American woman, has a child with Rafael Solano, who is Italian. The actors are Puerto Rican and Italian, respectively.

The Fosters, which was on air from 2013 to 2018, is yet another show that encapsulates racial and familial diversity. Terri Polo, who is white, plays Stef Adams Foster, and Sherri Saum, who is black, plays Lena Adams Foster. In the show, the Fosters are a lesbian couple with three children: Stef's biological son Brandon and two adopted children, Mariana and Jesus, who are both played by Latinx actors. They later adopt two more children, Callie and Jude, whom they foster at the onset of the show. Other shows that feature mixed-race adoption like in *Modern Family* and *The Fosters* include *Grey's Anatomy* (2005) and *This Is Us* (2016).

"It used to be that was the story," Trey said. "If they came to television, the story would be about this issue. Now it's no longer that." In other words, families, even families who deviate from what has long been considered the norm, are allowed to just be that: families.

Part Three

"Love is love is love."—Lin-Manuel Miranda, creator of In the Heights *and* Hamilton

CHAPTER TEN

Loving

From the Pew Research Center: Sixty-one percent of adults with parents or grandparents of different races do not consider themselves multiracial.

THE SUPREME COURT *LOVING V. VIRGINIA* decision gave Richard and Mildred Loving, a mixed-race couple, the right to marry in 1967. It has also redefined possibilities for people decades later, like David Pasteelnick, who is white, and Karl Stewart, who is black.

"Right off the bat, we were really conscious of it," said David about their race. "Whenever Karl sees a couple that's mixed-race, whether they're gay or straight, he goes, 'Oh, a Loving couple.' He always points them out to me."

In January 1959, Mildred Loving, a black and Native American woman who was then 20, and her husband Richard Loving, a white man who was 26, were arrested in a small town in central Virginia. Their marriage, performed in Washington, D.C., the previous June, was illegal under the state's Racial Integrity Act of 1924, and both of the Lovings were sentenced to a year in jail. They sued, and in 1967 the Supreme Court ruled the Racial Integrity Act unconstitutional, thereby allowing marriages between people of different races.

David and Karl have been together since February 7, 2015. That night, both of them had gone to a Mardi Gras party with a gay men's social group.

"We didn't know each other," said David. "I had actually gone to the party with some younger fellow that I had actually met a few weeks earlier and I brought him along to the party so I wasn't going by myself, and we just kind of met. I was talking to a bunch of people and suddenly he was there in the conversation. We just hit it off."

The next night, Karl invited David to dinner, where he made salmon. David and Karl married just over a year later, on December 16, 2016. Both men are in their fifties, wear shorts in the summer heat and have dark hair streaked with gray. On the roof of their Brooklyn apartment, David wore a tank top and sun hat, Karl a blue and white checked button-down and sunglasses.

"When I met him, there was no question in my mind that I was going to go down this road, whether it worked out or not, but it was like, 'Wow, okay, I'm dating a black guy again,'" said David. "There wasn't too much thought about what it means or how it might impact my life."

David and Karl moved to an apartment in Crown Heights together in April, 2017. The area is nearly 75 percent black and just over 19 percent white, according to the 2010 census data. The majority of the population is West Indian and African American, like Karl, but there are a significant number of Jews, like David, there, as well.

"Oddly enough, my very, very, very first boyfriend was African American, but then I mostly dated white guys after that, for a number of years," said David. "When I was actively dating, using websites and things as opposed to meeting people randomly, I certainly didn't restrict myself to anything. I'd say 70 percent of the men I dated were white, but I dated Asian guys. I dated Latino guys. It wasn't anything planned, and, in some ways, Karl was unexpected."

"For me, I originally dated black guys and it was interesting, because my first real relationship was with somebody for six and a half years and he was African American," Karl said. "And then after that, I was with somebody who was white for a while, but I didn't really think about it that way. When I was dating, I would look for very specific qualities in people, and that was the superseding idea. If it ended up being somebody African American or if it ended up being somebody white, it didn't really matter."

For Karl, it mattered less that David was white and more that he met his list of five criteria: He had to be out to his family, easy to talk to, financially solvent and comfortable on his own, sexy, and sober, or at least not fall-down drunk. "And race was not something that I was thinking about," he said.

However, Karl does believe that white men are out to their families more often. "In African American and West Indian

American communities, it's just harder for folks to be out in their families," he said. And, by virtue of his work, "I ended up being around a lot more white people than black people. It just happened that way. When I was an actuary, I was the only black actuary in the room. Even in human resources, there were only a couple black people. So, you end up spending more time with white people."

Even when he joined a group called Gay Men of African Descent, "I got a lot of support from that, but there was a strong sense within that community that you should date African Americans," said Karl. "There was a strong sort of reaction if someone in the community dated a white person. There was a sense that person was selling out. Very similar to that idea of acting white or wearing white clothes."

"Sometimes at our synagogue, we'll have interracial couples," David said. "And I don't say anything, but I want to go, 'Me, too!'" David said that his synagogue, while not an exclusively queer space, is "gay-welcoming." "We have a gay committee now that has events a couple times a year and whenever I'm there, people are like, 'Oh, is Karl coming today?' They all want to know about Karl."

Although they have found communities they love, such as David's synagogue, they said they do not always feel safe being together in public.

"In this neighborhood, we've not really walked hand in hand," said David about Crown Heights. "We'll go to the east village in Manhattan and, for the most part, feel comfortable. But we just started last month or so being comfortable enough to actually do that. You know, we don't want to cause trouble for ourselves."

"Even if I was by myself, even if David wasn't in the picture, they would be upset," said Karl, referring to the fact that many of the other black men in the area seem to not want to accept Karl because he is gay. "When I join with David and they see that connection, now they're like, 'There goes whatever respect I had for you because now you're with a white man.' It's like I've totally sold out."

Among older folks, particularly in the African American community, "I've always had a hypersensitive radar," Karl said. "I don't think it was as bad as when I first came to America in 1985, but I do see sort of the same dressing down, especially depending on how short my shorts are, especially in the summer." David laughed. Karl continued, "It's a millisecond transaction, especially with men, but women too. It's the sense of 'There goes the brother that could have been an upstanding member of our community, but now he's doing this other thing that we think isn't right.'"

At the same time, for David, being together is worth it. Or, as he put it, "As you get older, the amount of fucks you have to give dramatically reduce." When he met Karl, "I was rapidly approaching 50 and I didn't have very many left. It didn't occur to me that it could be an issue with my family. It didn't occur to me that it would be an issue with friends or employment, and it wasn't. I lost no friends and have no problems because of it."

"I think that's one of the yin and yangs between us," Karl said. "I want everybody in the world to say, 'Oh, great, you guys are together? That's wonderful.' David, as he explicitly said, has no fucks to give. It's a nice balance, because I learn to lean into his perspective with his whiteness."

"And he makes me kinder," said David.

"And I get to question, like, why do I care that this person walking toward us sees us?" said Karl. "In Manhattan, we definitely hold hands all the time, but I'm always hyper vigilant, looking to see if somebody from Bayside or Bensonhurst or some very Republican place far, far away is seeing us and what's their reaction. Part of me delights when they're kerfuffled about it and part of me looks for validation."

Karl added that simply holding hands is a thrill for him. "This is what every other straight, celebrated couple in New York City gets to do anywhere they are, so it's complicated, but it's always on my mind. As opposed to David, who's like, whatever."

"Ah, no, it's on my mind," David said.

With Karl's parents, though, it is harder to be delighted about their reaction to Karl and David's relationship. "They've shifted, but they still weren't able to come to the wedding," said Karl. "It felt as if it was still one step too far for them to support. But somebody told me anyone who needs to be at the wedding will be at the wedding, so that was comforting. Whoever needed to be there to support our love was there."

* * *

In just being with Karl, David said, "My worldview has expanded dramatically. I always like to think that I'm very liberal and aware, but I'm so much more so now. A lot of Karl's friends are my friends. Not all of them are people of color, but a lot of them are. I see their social media feeds and hear about their life experiences."

"Ironically, he's the one who posts on Facebook every time the police take an African American male and do very scary and horrible things," Karl said. "I refuse to pay attention to that feed because it's way too terrifying and personal for me. I'm just trying to not make it a reality."

"The fact that I have white privilege, that it simply exists, means it's my job to use my powers for good, to throw the weight of that at anything that might be negative," David said. "But there's the way it appears in the movies and the way it appears in real life, and the way it appears in real life is so much more subtle and unclear.

"My parents do a family vacation every year, including Karl because he is part of the family," he added. "We take a week and we go to different places, and last year we were in Williamsburg, Virginia. It was just post-election and the world was getting ugly. Nothing happened, but in my imagination, it comes up as something that might be a problem."

Since they started dating, David and Karl have spent extensive time with their in-laws. For David, this time has provided valuable lessons in privilege.

"Just spending time with Karl's family, it's an exercise in how I'm not the most important person in the room," David said. "Their traditions and their interactions and the way their family works is very different from what I'm used to, and it really is a lesson in how I'm not the baseline. It's good for me to live that and to understand, just to sit back and think, 'I have something to say and I'm not going to say it because it doesn't always matter that I have something to say.' Here, I'm the interloper, the visitor, the outsider of sorts."

David is a self-identified "Jersey boy." He was born in Scotch Plains, which is 77 percent white and 11 percent black as of 2010, and moved to Brooklyn in 2010. Karl was born in California, but spent most of his childhood in Jamaica, where both of his parents are from. Karl moved to New York in 1985 and spent time in Chelsea, Harlem, and Woodside, just to name a few places.

Jamaica is 92 percent black, 6 percent mixed, and just over 1 percent "other" and "unspecified." Karl's family is mostly Jamaican, except for his brother's wife, who is white.

"At the same time, though, his parents have been remarkably accommodating and kind with the whole kosher thing," said David. "They make me fish every time. It's really sweet."

As for Karl's sister-in-law, although Karl's mother was thrown the first time one of her sons began dating a white person, "She's been in the family ten years, a very long time," David said. "She's got her street cred now. She's earned her stripes and everything, gotten the trust of his parents. I'm still the novice, so I'm in a different world and I need to roll with that. Their traditions and their interactions and the way their family works is very different from what I'm used to."

Karl feels similarly about being with David's family. "I've always been an anthropology student of life. Even in my career, I'm an HR person. The designers are designing and I'm just observing, as though I'm watching an anthill do its thing and going, 'Let's make sure the ants don't kill each other.' So, I'm very comfortable going into his family situations where there are 80 people and I'm still trying to figure out how it all works."

"He's a real trooper," David said. "It's terrifying. My father's side of the family is very close-knit, so we have an enormous Seder every year. Karl has been coming for three years now, I think, and everyone loves him."

He continued, "Also, it's a really mixed family. We have Jewish Asian family, Jewish African American. Other people in our family have moved away from Judaism, but they still come to the Seder. We have a Greek Orthodox minister in our family now. So, it's a big ol' stew. It's always felt intrinsic. It's an important part and Karl's been very respectful."

"I've always found that fascinating, so it's exciting for me," said Karl. "I have my own ways of feeling autonomy and control in those situations, and I'm even learning to adjust those. Like, I'm always wanting to help clean or to do other physical, tangible things. That's always been my thing, is to figure out the code that works in this society or group or organization of people, and I make myself useful. That's always been my way."

Karl's first Thanksgiving with David's family, David said, David's dad asked Karl to make the turkey. "I just ended up following the recipe," said Karl.

"He was brilliant, though," David said.

"Just gotta make it happen," Karl said.

Even with the contentious political climate, David believes that, "Overall, at least in New York, we're in a very good time to be in this relationship. Hopefully, things will get even better, but if there was a time for me to be with someone of a different race, this is the place and time to do it. It doesn't stop me in any way. In one of the theater groups I'm in, there's already two or three interracial couples in the troop. It works. That's the long and short of it."

"I think there's difference in two human beings period, even if they both grew up in the same town from third grade all the way through college," said Karl. "There is a difference. On some level, there's a lot of yin and yang between David and I, but it's not about two halves becoming a whole. It's about two separate human beings joining in a relationship."

Karl added, "It didn't matter what the outside package was. It mattered what the internal things were. Those, I think, are just a perfect fit."

CHAPTER ELEVEN

"I Guess I'm More Japanese Than You"

From the American Psychological Association: Multiracial children are now the largest demographic under the age of 18 in the US.

"RACE. WOW." LYNDA GOMI, A white American woman, turned to her husband, Kazuhiro, who is Japanese and from Japan, and continued. "So, I guess, from our experience, I would say culture is the bigger difference. And that could be socioeconomic culture, or that could be Japanese culture, American culture."

Lynda and Kazuhiro Gomi sat at their dining room table in Laura Generale's hometown of Dobbs Ferry, New York. Lynda and Kazuhiro met while Lynda was teaching in Japan, several years ago. Every year, more than 450,000 US citizens marry non-US citizens, according to the US Department of Commerce, or about

0.14 percent of the population. The Ministry of Health cites that in Japan, the number of Japanese citizens to marry non-Japanese citizens was about 21,488 in 2013, or about 0.02 percent.

"I think your culture has nothing to do with your DNA," Kazuhiro added. "It's just the environment creating human characters. When I hear race, I think it's more scientific. For example, I think there are some specific diseases that certain races are more susceptible to. So those things, to me, are race."

The couple has moved back and forth several times since marrying, though they have been in the US, in Dobbs Ferry, for more than a decade. While about 81 percent of the population in Dobbs Ferry is white, the next biggest population, Asian, is just under 8 percent. Japan, on the other hand, is racially homogeneous, nearly 99 percent Japanese. Smaller populations include Koreans, Chinese, and Filipinos, according to an article in *Asia Times.*

"Well, I think both cultures have small-minded people," said Lynda. "But Japanese culture in particular focuses on who's in the group and who's outside of the group, so pointing at people and identifying them as outside of the group is kind of the norm. Children would always point at me and say 'foreigner' or 'outside person.'"

"Living in America, you have to act like an American," said Kazuhiro. "That's important." At the same time, Kazuhiro said, "The US culture is obviously more of a melting pot, especially in New York. I think it's important to have your identity. Everybody, I think, living here, has their own identity."

In terms of the culture, "I think that the US has more culture allowing, and also people are really proud of that ethnic heritage," he said. "That's definitely very different."

He added, "In Japan, if some American or some other people came to live in Tokyo and tried to stand out, saying 'I'm an American,' probably the people around them would take it differently and probably more negatively. I'm learning that that's quite different here."

"But remember what happened in Michigan?" Lynda asked. "We were visiting my parents up in this small little town in Michigan. I kept saying, 'We're going to get to America and you're just going to feel so welcome. You're just going to look like everybody else.' I had grown up in a much bigger city and had moved to this smaller town."

She continued, "The first time we go out of the house, we're in this grocery store, a man comes up to him and says, 'Are you Japanese? I fought in World War II.' It wasn't in a negative way. He just wanted to share his experience. I guess he was there after the war and he met people there and he wasn't being negative. But I was like, 'Wait a minute, how come you're being pushed into the outside category? This isn't supposed to be happening.'"

Both in the US and in Japan, Lynda is a teacher. She said she always tries to push the boundaries of what it means to be Japanese in Japan or American in the US.

"When I was teaching junior high, high school, we would have this discussion about what it means to be Japanese," she said. "And I would say, 'Well how long have you lived here?' They would say, '15 years,' and I would say 'I've lived here longer, so I guess I'm more Japanese than you are.' And they would say, 'Oh, no, no, no, no, you can't be more Japanese.' So, I kind of like to push those boundaries, to get people to think beyond the 'You don't look like me, so you're outside.'"

When Lynda went to work in Japan as a teacher, she was only given one instruction from her parents: come home single. Though she failed to do so, her parents forgave her as soon as they met Kazuhiro.

"They immediately fell in love. They liked him better than me right away," she joked.

Kazuhiro's parents were very accepting of Lynda, as well. Although it was hard for both sets of parents to know that their children would be spending a lot of time in another country, Kazuhiro's parents did have experience interacting with people outside of Japan.

"My father was in international companies, so he was very exposed to other cultures," Kazuhiro said.

"He traveled," said Lynda. "And your mom went with him."

Kazuhiro nodded. "Yeah, my mom went with him for business trips and stuff. So they were pretty exposed. They actually liked to have American college students do the homestay."

"That's how we met," said Lynda. "My college roommate's brother stayed at his house."

"My mom once told me, I don't know if she remembers, 'You can have a non-Japanese wife, I don't care. Do whatever you like,'" Kazuhiro added.

Soon after they married, Lynda and Kazuhiro had their first child, a boy they named Kiyota. Several years later, they had a daughter, a girl named Aila. Both children spent most of their early years back and forth, spending the year in Yokohama, Japan, and summers in the US.

"Kazu's job at that time was with a domestic telephone company and, so we would be living in Japan," said Lynda. "We decided that we would speak English in the home, and when we were outside, we would speak Japanese. His parents lived very close, so when they were around, we would speak Japanese around them. We would get the kids to the US every summer, so a huge part of our budget was dedicated to that airplane fare. And my parents had space that we could stay in while we were here."

Though Kazuhiro's job had been in Japan, Lynda knew she wanted her children to come to the US for college.

"Japanese gets you this great foundation of facts and knowledge, but then college doesn't help you use it," she said. "So, that whole critical, analytical thinking piece that's so important a focus in Western schools, I wanted my kids to have that."

Both Lynda and Kazuhiro agree that it was easy for them to flip back and forth between languages, at least compared to other couples they have known.

"I belonged to a group of women married to Japanese men," said Lynda. "There were a lot of different situations, so in many cases, the husbands hated English and let that attitude be known. So, we certainly didn't have that. We both shared positive perspectives with the kids."

"In that regard, I think we both wanted the kids to be bilingual, bicultural," said Kazuhiro.

Lynda added, "We both respected each other's culture and we wanted our children to have both."

Though their children are now adults, Lynda remembered a time when Kiyota had to cope with bullying from other students.

"I remember Kiyo coming home from first grade and a boy was teasing him," she said. "The boy was calling him 'French underwear,' which sounds a little bit like 'French bread' in Japanese. And I just burst out laughing. It was so stupid because, well, we're not French, first of all. And I think I've always been so happy that my response was to laugh rather than getting crazy and blowing up because than it would have made him tense. And this kid actually ended up being his best friend by sixth grade. The two of them were inseparable."

Kazuhiro and Lynda also said that while the children were very conscious of being mixed from a young age, it's hard to actively be both Asian and white.

"Whenever they would be walking with me, I would be getting pointed at which means they would be getting pointed at," said Lynda about Japan.

"I would say, yeah, they were pretty conscious about it," Kazuhiro added.

"One of my regrets is that they haven't gotten to the point where they really are both," said Lynda. "Growing up in Japan, they were Japanese. When they were here, they had English-speaking friends. They didn't have Japanese friends. So, they were either one or the other. And that blending didn't really happen."

* * *

Looking to the future, both Lynda and Kazuhiro cannot help but think about the Trump administration, although Kazuhiro is more optimistic than Lynda.

"One person I don't think can turn this whole ship to the wreck," said Kazuhiro. "There's definitely a whole system. The US has managed to maintain the checks and balances."

"Well, we thought we did," Lynda said. "We're discovering that we didn't."

"I'm not so paranoid about my own individual situation," said Kazuhiro. "I'm more worried about the whole world. I think I'm most worried about the reputation about the United States of America from the rest of the world. I think people used to have all the respect and admiration for the US. I think that is going away every day."

"Every tweet," Lynda joked.

"I think that's really hard to regain if you lose it," said Kazuhiro. "It takes more than four years to do so." Of the Japanese government, Kazuhiro commented, "I think the Japanese government has no choice but following the US government right now because of the North Korea situation. We need someone to protect the country, so the Japanese government has no choice. I think the Japanese people in general, no one supports Trump."

Lynda and Kazuhiro are both involved in the Japanese American Association of New York. More recently, the organization has become focused on what is happening with Muslims in the US, largely because of Trump's proposed Muslim ban. Though his ban did not take place, Trump has also suggested a Muslim registry, which would mean the estimated 3.3 million Muslims living in the US would have to become a part of a public registry according to Pew. This has been compared to Hitler's keeping track of the Jewish residents in Nazi Germany during World War II.

Many also fear that a Muslim registry would lead to mass internment, such as with the Japanese Americans in the US during the same time period. This has opened the floodgates for the organization, and the Japanese-American community as a whole, to become politically active.

"Their relatives were interned during World War II, so they are identifying with the Islamic community and reaching out to the Islamic community," said Lynda. "After the war, the families were ashamed that they had been put into a concentration camp and all of their possessions taken away from them. You put it behind you by being quiet. They didn't have conversations with their children, but now their grandchildren and great grandchildren are saying, 'Come on, tell us, tell us.'"

She continued, "So now, in this environment, they're going back to their relatives and the relatives are like, 'You want to hear my story? But my story's not important.' It's really important because this is going to happen again. They start telling this story to the family that they've never told before. So, very exciting."

Even further into the future, Lynda and Kazuhiro are looking forward to seeing what Kiyota and Aila do with their lives. Kiyota lives in Boston, Massachusetts, which is 46 percent non-Hispanic white and 9 percent Asian as of 2015. Aila lives in Cleveland, Ohio, 33 percent white and less than 2 percent Asian. The largest population in Cleveland is black—53 percent based on the 2010 census.

Both Kiyota and Aila ended up going to school in the US, just as Lynda had planned. Kiyota went to Carlton College for his undergraduate degree, which is 62 percent white and nearly 9 percent Asian, and Boston University for graduate school, which is 40 percent white and 14 percent Asian among the undergraduate students. Aila went to Case Western Reserve University, which is 50 percent white and 20 percent Asian.

Both Kiyota and Aila's choices to stay in the US for college may have been influenced by the fact that, once the family moved to the US for good, they spoke almost entirely English. Lynda said she gave up speaking Japanese in the house after she realized she was speaking it more than Kazuhiro or the kids.

"We used to be really good about it when his parents were around, and we would speak in Japanese around them," she said. "Maybe not so much anymore. Language is a habit, and once you get comfortable with your habit, changing really takes some serious determination. Kiyo did take Japanese in college, but in his career has not used Japanese or sought that as a way to give him a step up and be ahead of everybody else."

"I'm hoping that the both of them maintain some culture from Japan and implement it into their family traditions," said Kazuhiro. "I believe they will. That's what I'm hoping for."

"Definitely the food side," Lynda said. "But interestingly, I think Japanese New Year is more important than Christmas to them. Christmas was just our small little family group. It wasn't a whole big craziness. But New Year's was going to visit their great uncle and great aunt and distant cousins. So that—well, again, the whole culture was celebrating Japanese New Year. Kiyo is making a point to come home for New Year's."

CHAPTER TWELVE

The Rainbow

From the Pew Research Center: About 30 percent of adults in the US with parents or grandparents of different races have changed the way they have described their own race over the years.

WHEN 19-YEAR-OLD SIMONE THOMAS, who is West African, met Alanna Ramos, who is Puerto Rican, she never imagined they would move in together six years later, and get engaged just two years after that.

"We met on a summer internship," said Simone. "I usually call it the gayest way: we met at a softball internship."

Both women had the Posse scholarship through the Posse Foundation. Simone received her scholarship through Babson College in Wellesley, Massachusetts, which is 38 percent white, 10 percent Hispanic, and 5 percent black. Babson is considered very diverse, according to College Simply, just like Cornell University, Guilford College, George Washington University, and Stony Brook University. Simone later went to Columbia University for her journalism degree, which is just 37 percent white and about 7 percent black among its undergraduate students, also ranked high in diversity.

Alanna's Posse scholarship came through Trinity College in Hartford, Connecticut, which is 65 percent white, 6 percent black and 7 percent Hispanic. When they met, both women had just finished their first years in college.

"Someone told me that there was going to be another Posse scholar interning, and I thought I'd keep an eye out for them," Simone said. "Obviously, I didn't talk to her because I was shy as hell and still am, but one day she came up to me and I had these bracelets on that were rainbow colored. I was just missing one, a yellow one, and she pointed it out. So that told me that she noticed the bracelets and might know that I'm queer. That's how we first started actually talking and communicating."

Simone, who is now 27, sat on the couch wearing a white crop top and jeans while Alanna sat on the rug in a blue button-up shirt and jeans.

"It was the first thing I said to her," Alanna said. "You're missing one. The first thing I said because I was nervous, too."

"And then maybe a week or two passed, and she ended up getting me the yellow one," Simone continued, twisting the yellow bracelet she still wears on her wrist. "She went around town to find it. And ever since then, she's completed my rainbow."

Both woman drank lemon water while Jennifer Lopez played softly in the background. "She likes that song," Alanna remarked of Simone. "I don't even like that song. Go figure. I think J. Lo sings horribly in Spanish."

Simone rolled her eyes. "Okay, Alanna."

"I love J. Lo, though."

Simone laughed. "Jesus," she said.

For Alanna, who was born and raised in Chicago, the internship was her first time in New York City. According to 2010 US census data, Chicago is approximately 33 percent black, 32 percent non-Hispanic white, and 29 percent Hispanic or Latinx. Now, Alanna and Simone live in the Bronx, which is about 54 percent Hispanic and Latinx, 43 percent black, and 11 percent non-Hispanic white as of 2013.

"Once I did the internship in New York for the summer and Simone and I started dating, that's when I decided, after my time at Trinity that I was going to move to New York," Alanna said.

"She likes to say that she came here for me, but I don't want that kind of pressure on me," Simone joked.

Alanna laughed. "Mostly it was that, but also it was for my job."

Alanna is a police officer, a profession that has few people of color, which Simone believes complicates Alanna's relationship with Simone's black mother. In 2016, the Criminal Justice Bureau reported that only 16 percent of all police officers in the US are African American. The same holds true for the New York Police Department, even though African Americans represent 23 percent of New York City.

"I feel like we have a really complicated relationship around Alanna because there are many layers," said Simone. "My mom can be prejudiced to people who are Latino. If Alanna were black, I think my mom would have been a little more okay. But then on top of that, Alanna is a cop. That came later. She wasn't an officer when we first started dating. My mom hasn't had the most positive experiences with the police and she doesn't trust the police. So, that just made it harder for her."

Simone's mother didn't know about Simone and Alanna's relationship until a year or so after they got together. Although Simone dated some girls in high school, she was only out to a few close friends.

"I finally came out when I was dating Alanna in 2010," Simone said. "No, actually it was next summer. After almost a year of dating, I decided I was going to tell my mom. Alanna was important to me. So, I had to explain to my mom that Alanna is not just my friend, she's my girlfriend. My mom took it well, which was shocking. She basically said, 'I'm happy with whoever makes you happy.'"

"My family had known about my queer status, if you will, since I was 15," said Alanna. "That's when I kind of came out. It was a really rough time because my family, they kicked me out. I went away for college, which was the best thing. It actually improved the relationship with them. Simone was the first girlfriend I ever had that I told my parents about, since I was dating somebody I really cared for. This was six months after we had met."

Alanna's mom was surprised about two things when Alanna introduced her to Simone: that Alanna was in a serious relationship at all, since she had never introduced her parents to anyone she had dated before, and that Simone was not Latina.

"She mentioned, you know, 'Oh, I didn't know that you didn't like Spanish girls,'" Alanna said. "It's not that I don't like Spanish girls, it's just that I like her, and she happens to not be Spanish."

Alanna's mother is from Puerto Rico, while her father was born and raised in Chicago, like Alanna. "But his parents are from Puerto Rico," Alanna said. "Our ancestry is all Puerto Rican."

"All of it?" Simone said.

"Most of it."

Simone laughed. "She doesn't want to claim the Spaniards."

"There's a small percent of Spanish in my family," Alanna said. "We don't really associate with that side of the family—"

"The colonizers," Simone added.

"—just because there was a lot of pain there. My grandmother doesn't like to talk about it, so out of respect for her, we've always identified with Puerto Rican culture. She never really had the opportunity to get to know the Spanish side. I've been to Puerto Rico multiple times, but I was born in Chicago."

Simone's parents, like Alanna's mom, are immigrants. Her mother is from Guinea and her father is from Liberia, though Simone was raised in Brooklyn. The census estimates that, as of 2015, Brooklyn is about 36 percent non-Hispanic white, 35 percent black, and 20 percent Hispanic or Latinx.

"For a long, long time, she just referred to Alanna as my friend, never said her name or anything," Simone remembered. "But then, one Thanksgiving probably two years ago or three years ago, it was just me, my mom, Alanna, my sister and her boyfriend, so just the five of us, and she referred to Norman, my sister's boyfriend, as my sister's friend. In that moment, we all looked at each other like, 'Okay, I guess everyone's a friend.'"

Although the two come from different backgrounds, Alanna said that now, "I forget we're interracial. It's not until I introduce her to one of my friends and they ask if she speaks Spanish. And I say she understands a little bit of it, and they'll say, 'Oh cool, I haven't met many black people who speak Spanish.' And then I'm like, oh yeah, Simone's black."

"Most of the time, I don't think about it unless someone points it out, and most people don't," Simone said. "Except, one instance I was at work, and someone came over and saw a picture of Alanna on my desk, and they were like, 'Oh, I kind of imagined you'd have a black girlfriend who looks like Lauryn Hill or something.' They didn't think at all. I said, 'That's interesting. Why would you assume that?' They just assumed it."

Simone said that, because she cares about issues in the black community, people "Think I should be dating someone in my race. It's like Jesse from *Grey's Anatomy*," referring to the character Jackson Avery, played by Jesse Williams. Williams is African American, Seminole, and Swedish.

"He's always talking about Black Lives Matter and everything, and he married a white woman," Simone continued. "People were like, 'Whoa, what are you doing? How can you possibly be woke or whatever and not date another black person?' I think that's why people assume that my partner would be black."

At the same time, Simone said she grew up around a lot of Hispanic culture, so being around Alanna's family does not feel like an adjustment. "I love it," she said. "I attribute it to my mom, but I grew up listening to Spanish music. I grew up listening to bachata and merengue and I grew up in a house where we kept the radio on Spanish-speaking stations. I grew up with the food. So, when it came to being with Alanna, I didn't feel like it was totally jarring. I knew the songs that she played and I knew the foods that she ate."

* * *

Alanna proposed to Simone in May 2018. At the top of the High Line, an elevated park in Manhattan, Simone's friends and family, her brother and twin sister, each handed her a rose. "I wanted the people you love to give you flowers," Alanna told her later. Alanna stood at the end of the line, waiting to propose. Simone said yes.

"I pulled my parents aside individually and told my father first that I was going to propose to Simone," said Alanna. "When it came to getting married, my dad was overprotective and concerned, as a parent would be, but what's more, he kept reminding me that if it's something I wanted to do, if I'm happy he's happy and he likes Simone. That meant a lot to me.

"My mom loves Simone and has a great relationship with her," she continued. "But when I told her the morning before I flew out to come back to New York, I told her I was going to be proposing to Simone, and she just reminded me that she does care about Simone and that she's happy for me, but that this is not the life that she expected for me.

Alanna asked her parents if they would be willing to come to New York for the proposal and meet Simone's mother. Both of them said no.

"My mom just started making excuses as to why she couldn't come," Alanna said. "She kept saying, 'It's not that I don't want to be there, it's that I can't because of X, Y, and Z.' Simone will tell you that I'm the first person that, when someone needs something at home, or if there's something going on, I'm the first to fly out and be there. The one time I ask something of them, they didn't show up. It was really hurtful, and it still kind of hurts."

Simone has not yet told her mother she is engaged.

"Her mom texted her the day of the proposal," Simone said of Alanna. "And I could see how happy she was for her, but Alanna was kind of heartbroken because it was a text message, and she wanted her mom to be here. I didn't want that. If anything, when I tell people I'm engaged to my partner of eight years, I want them to be excited and happy for me. I didn't want to have to think, oh, are they going to be okay or is this something they are going to be concerned about. I don't want any of that. I think that's why I haven't told my mom yet. I'm not prepared for anything less than excitement and happiness."

"Especially with us being together eight years," said Alana. "It's not like we've been together for one or two years and want to get married. We live together and have meals together."

"I think it's hard because when you're trying to become a legitimate family, it's like we're disrupting whatever paradigm of family they've had," Simone said. "And it's coming from your family, which is so weird."

Simone laughed. "It's going to be interesting talking about having kids with them," she said.

Simone and Alanna would prefer to adopt—under no circumstances does Alanna want to be pregnant—and said that they would prefer to adopt biracial children, preferably children who are Latinx and black, like them.

"Alanna is going to have a kid walking down the street with a darker complexion," said Simone. "What are they going to be thinking about her? Did you adopt this child or do you have a black husband? For me, will they think I'm the kid's nanny? I've thought about this for years, what our family will end up looking like and how we'll be treated."

She added, "If I'm looking at a child, I would want a child that looks like me. That's what I would want. But then, I would also want a child that looks like us."

"So there would be no way you would want a child that doesn't look like us at all?" Alanna asked.

"I mean, I could. I'm open to that, too," Simone said. "I remember, you said once that you wanted a white baby. I thought that would be weird."

"See, you thought that was weird, but I thought it would be totally normal," Alanna said.

Simone laughed. "That would be weird," she insisted. "I mean, think about it. I have to think about it from my perspective. I'm going to be a black woman walking around with a white baby."

"Yeah, and I'm a Puerto Rican woman walking around with a white baby," Alanna said.

"Who has a very fair complexion," Simone said. "It would be different. People would assume that's your baby."

"Okay," Alanna said. "That's fair."

"I guess I thought it was weird only because I was looking at it from my perspective and how hard it would be," said Simone. "But even then, if we end up finding a child we love, no matter what they are, then I'm happy with that, too."

With a biracial child, "I'll be able to feel like there's a connection there because that'll be possibly the closest to what we could have," said Alanna. "That's the hard part about not being able to have babies on our own."

She added, "They don't have to be Puerto Rican and West African. That's very specific and that's hard to find. But if we can at least have a Latino and black child, that would be helpful for us."

They joke that their family would be like *The Fosters*, the TV show in which an interracial couple adopts children of various races. Simone remarks that they have actually seen several mixed-race lesbian couples in popular media.

"That's something I've always picked up on," said Simone. "There's Robin Roberts and her wife, who's white—"

"Who we've met!" Alanna added.

"—Wanda Sykes and her wife," Simone continued. "Shows like the *The L Word*, one of the main characters is biracial and the other is white. More often than not, you see mixed families when it comes to lesbian couples. For *The Fosters*, that was awesome. And it was such a great representation and such a great show."

At the same time, many of these couples usually have one distinct difference from Alanna and Simone: one of the people is black, and the other is white.

"I don't know too many interracial couples who are not white and black," said Alanna. "When we started dating, we were the couple I knew who wasn't white and black, but mixed people of color. So, that was cool, because a lot of people started recognizing us as that couple. A lot of time in media, you'll see predominantly a black person and a white person dating. You don't really see an Asian person and a black person, for example."

"Even when people look at us sometimes, though, they see that," Simone said. "They see a white person and a black person. When we were living in Brooklyn sometimes, on the subway, we'd get the dirtiest of looks from older people of color, older black women, staring at us. And I'll get dirty looks at me, pointed, like I'm selling out because I'm not dating a black person. But would they be happy if I was dating a black woman? So, I don't know where there's winning with people."

Even at Pride, Simone said, "This black guy said something. Like, 'You gotta love your people' or something. It took me a while to realize he was saying that because I'm a black woman not dating a black person, regardless of gender. So, in that context it gets harder, because I don't want to have to stop and explain that Alanna is a person of color."

More recently, Alanna and Simone had been having what Alanna calls "hard talks" about what it means to go into predominantly Latinx spaces or spaces that are mostly black. Although one partner may enjoy being in her community, the other may struggle to figure out where she fits in.

"We went to a party with Alanna's friends and I was the only black person," said Simone. "The majority of the people there were Latinx, Spanish-speaking, everything, and I really felt left out. But there was another instance where there was a party that was mostly African people and I asked if Alanna wanted to come, and that started a whole conversation about how we are in these spaces, if we were comfortable, because we should probably talk about it. We're still figuring that out. We're figuring it out right now."

"As an interracial couple in very diverse spaces, it's fine because it's given that it's a diverse space," said Alanna. "But if we're in a community or an area where it's tailored more to one partner than the other, I want my partner to feel comfortable in that space that is meant for me, but I don't want to overshadow or be extra if the space is not for me. So we've been talking about that—"

"—what it means to say the space is not for me, but I'm here because the space is for my partner," Simone said.

"Even after eight years of dating and eight years of being interracial, there are still certain moments where we want to be supportive and for the other person to have a good time in these spaces, but it's challenging because there's a level of comfort that one person has that the other just doesn't," said Alanna. "So, how do we become compassionate to that person in those situations while still holding them accountable?"

"And it's not just in social settings," Simone said. "We were in Brooklyn living together in our first apartment in Brownsville, which is a very black neighborhood. Alanna walked down the street and people thought she was a teacher or a random person coming into the neighborhood. Because they thought, 'Why else would this light-skinned person be in this black neighborhood unless you're teaching at one of the elementary schools?'"

Now, Simone said they live in a predominantly Latinx neighborhood. "We keep moving into different spaces with each other," she said. "Now I understand how Alanna felt walking down the street. But to a certain extent, I feel comfortable, because I could be Latinx." Simone turned to Alanna. "You could never be black. I mean, you could, but no one would think that. I could be mistaken for Afro-Latina. With you, that would never happen."

Ultimately, though both women were glad they can have these conversations. "The one thing I loved about Alanna when we first started dating was that Alanna never said, 'I'm colorblind. I don't see color,'" Simone said. "I think I would have been completely turned off. I wouldn't have talked to her."

She continued, "I couldn't date someone who says 'I don't see your color. I don't see how you interact with the world. I don't see how you interact with other people. I don't see how the world sees you.' That's not love. I don't think that's love at all. You're not seeing me, completely me, if you don't see my race and see how that affects whatever our love is."

CHAPTER THIRTEEN

The Best Part

From the US Census Bureau: Ninety-two percent of people who reported being more than one race identified as biracial, or exactly two races.

JULIAN HUMES, A BLACK MAN from Durham, North Carolina, was in sixth grade when he first thought about the implications of being involved with someone of another race. That was when Julian, now 22, told his father that a white classmate had a crush on him.

"The first thing he said was, 'That's nice and all, but not everyone's parents have the same views about who their kids associate with,'" Julian said.

Now, Julian is dating Devon Murphy-Anderson, a 23-year-old white woman from Maine, which she said is "The whitest state in America." The two started going out in 2016.

"It isn't the easiest thing, but it's been worth it for us," said Julian. "The struggles of being different from one another and from the majority of couples around only makes your relationship stronger. I think it's opened my mind to different cultures."

For Julian, being black is an important and positive part of his identity. At the same time, being black in the US can also pose risks that white people do not have to deal with in their day-to-day lives. Black US Americans make up about 38 percent of the prison population at federal institutions and the same number at state prisons, even though black people make up less than 13 percent of the total US population. This means that black people are more than five times as likely to be incarcerated in the US as white people.

In 11 states, black people represent more than half the prison population. The American Civil Liberties Union reported that one in three black boys and one in six Latinos can expect to spend time in prison in their lives. The number is one in 17 for white boys. Often, these are for low-level drug offenses, even though black and white Americans use drugs at approximately the same rate.

In 2014, Mic reported that there were more black prisoners in the US prison system by percent than there were during apartheid in South Africa. They also noted that one in every 28 US American children grows up with a parent behind bars. The majority of them are black and brown, since that is who makes up the prison population.

"Because of my upbringing as a black male, as I've grown up, I've come to understand race with a negative connotation," said

Julian. "That's because a lot of things that have happened to myself and people I love have been solely because of race."

Black people are also more likely to be targeted by the police than white people. Of the 987 people killed by police officers in the US in 2017, 20 percent were black, according to the Washington Post database. Other sources, such as *The Root* and *Salon*, estimate the number of people killed by police is closer to 1,129.

According to the 2010 census, Durham is approximately 42 percent white and 40 percent black. Brunswick, Maine, where Devon grew up, is approximately 93 percent white and less than 1 percent black. Julian and Devon agree that this affected their backgrounds and initial understanding of race.

"I think sometimes we have a hard time understanding where the other one is coming from because we've had such vastly different childhoods and experiences," said Devon, who had moved to New York during the 2018 election to work for Liuba Grechen Shirley, a Democratic congressional candidate in the second congressional district of Long Island, New York.

Devon's district is made up of mostly Suffolk County, which is 75 percent non-Hispanic white and 7 percent black, and a small part of Nassau County, which is 66 percent non-Hispanic white and 11 percent black. On November 6, 2018, Shirley lost to Republican incumbent Peter King, who has been accused of racism in the past for using an anti-Asian slur on television in 2016 and for a history of Islamophobic comments.

"I think we've realized in our relationship that those different experiences are somehow related to race," Devon continued. "We have to talk about everyday things more than most couples, I think. But I also think that can be an advantage because it forces us to communicate."

Much of their conversations about race come about from day-to-day interactions with other people, according to Devon. "Usually, it's older white people in restaurants," she said. "I think I've realized that as a white person dating a black person, that people approach me about it more than they approach him."

She added, "Sometimes it pisses me off because I feel like the only thing that matters about our relationship is that Julian's black. That makes me upset for so many reasons, but mostly because we have an incredible relationship that deserves to be recognized for many other reasons."

Although they are young, they have already started thinking about what it will be like to have mixed-race children. While Julian hopes overall views on race will have changed in the US from when he was growing up, Devon is struggling with these ideas for the first time.

"Hopefully, I won't have to speak to my children in the same capacity as I was spoken to about race when I was young," said Julian. "That's not because they may not be as brown as me, but because hopefully societal views of race will continue to change for the better. But yes, I think that because my children will be mixed race that I will still have to point out the advantages and disadvantages of being non-white."

"Race is so complicated, especially in America," Devon said. "I think a great place to start those conversations is with history, because it provides a context. But as a parent I think I'll also be very aware of the timing of those conversations. Children are taught racial identities, stereotypes, and boundaries. It's not something we are born knowing. So, I wouldn't want to force my children to have that awareness before it was necessary."

In spite of the difficulties, the couple said that the good outweighs the bad.

"It isn't the easiest thing but it's been worth it for us," said Julian. "Getting looks from people and feeling unwelcome becomes normal. But the struggles of being different from one another and from the majority of couples around you only makes your relationship stronger."

"I mean, I really love him, and he happens to be black," Devon said. "So, the best part is completely unrelated to race. It's that I get to love him and be with him."

CHAPTER FOURTEEN

Biology, History, and White Privilege

From the Pew Research Center: The median age of mixed-race US Americans is 19, while the median age of single-race Americans is 38.

TO KARL JACOBY, A PROFESSOR of history and ethnic studies at Columbia University, the mix of confusion, love, and frustration people have for their mixed-race identities, whether familial or individual, makes perfect sense. Karl, who has taught at Columbia since 2012, has focused on westward expansion and race in his classes. In the fall of 2017, he taught a class called Troubling the Color Line, about passing as other races, interracial marriage, and questions of ethnic ambiguity.

Karl believes that "The central element for a lot of American historians has been thinking about the black-white divide." However, he is "Trying to expand that to include Native Americans, Latinos, and Asian Americans, as well."

Karl is white, with dark hair and eyes. He is married to the Korean American essayist and novelist Marie Myong-Ok Lee. Together, they have a son, Jason. On a winter afternoon, he sat in an office piled high with books about history, race, and the United States. "If you're teaching American history, it's impossible not to run up against the foundational role that race played in structuring American society," he said.

In his view, one of the few constants in the way race has been used in the US over the years has been to help whites. As an example, he cited what is known as "the one-drop law," or the idea that anyone with even one drop of African American blood is automatically considered African American. On the other hand, Native Americans must have a certain amount of Native ancestry to qualify for that designation.

In the first example, this policy kept available a sizable enslavable population for white slave owners. In the second, limiting the Native population in the US also limits the number of reparations the government has to pay to the community.

"These ideas seem to point in really different directions," Karl said. "But I'd say the one commonality is that both of those ways of thinking about race tend to benefit white people."

He notes that the concept of race has changed throughout the history of the US, even in public records. African Americans were counted in the US census when they came to the US, but there was a separate section for enslaved people and their names were not included. Native Americans were not considered citizens in the US until the 1920s.

Along that same vein, when Italian and Irish people came to the US for the first time, they were not always considered white. Arab people, on the other hand, were considered white for a long time. Though that has changed in practice, Arab Americans still count as "white" on the US census.

Because of this ever-changing series of definitions, Karl, along with many other social scientists, hold that race is a social construct, meaning it has no biological basis.

At the same time, he cautions that the concept of race continues to affect the lives of everyone in the US. "People often think that if you take the constructionist view, you're saying that race isn't real," he said. "But you're only saying it isn't biologically real. It is socially real. It has powerful consequences in terms of life opportunities, in terms of wealth, and in terms of educational opportunities." In other words, while race has real-life consequences, these consequences have only come about because we have decided that race matters and not because of biology.

"The early 19th century is when ideas of race as a biological reality began to emerge," said Karl. "Over time, these ideas have shifted in the sense that people used to create a lot of different races, so they would talk about Jews as a race and Italians as a race and whatnot. By the early 20th century, these began to collapse, so you're seeing more of whites as one group."

Ever since 1492, when white, European settlers came to what would come to known as the New World and began to subjugate Native Americans and, half a century later, to kidnap and enslave Africans, US Americans have been producing mixed-race children as well as the scourge of racism.

Over the years, many have thought that intermarriage would be the solution to racism, but Karl disagrees, referring to the famous Supreme Court case, *Loving v. Virginia*, to make his point, the case in which the Supreme Court ruled all state laws banning interracial marriage unconstitutional.

According to the Associated Press, between 1970 and 2005, marriages between black and white people increased more than six times, from 65,000 in 1970 to 422,000 in 2005. Karl, however, does not believe this is enough to have "produced some sort of non-racist utopia."

"Some people think that the solution to all our racial problems is intermarriage, that if we all just intermarry with each other there will be no whites, there will be no blacks, there will be no Asians," he said. "This is something that people have been talking about for a long time, but if you look at American history, there's been a tremendous history of racial mixing. All these groups have actually been having relationships ever since 1492." In spite of this, racism has continued to exist in US American culture.

The steady stream of racial bias has continued into the 21st century. The 2015 US Pew study found that only 22 percent of US adults considered the growing number of mixed-race marriages a good thing, down from 39 percent in 2014. About 11 percent said such marriages are a bad thing, and 65 percent believe they do not make a difference.

Of the discussion surrounding mixed-race US Americans, Karl said, "It's come about mainly because the census has started allowing people to check more than one box and race works in very interesting ways in the US, which is to say that different mixtures are interpreted differently."

For Karl, the real problem is that defining people as "mixed-race" still emphasizes differences based on race.

"The challenge about using the idea of mixed race is that it still reifies the concept of race," he said. "If you're saying you're mixed race, you're saying there are these two or three or whatever different races and this person is mixing these things that are definable, real things together in one body. So, in some ways, the very term doesn't get you outside of these problematic ways of thinking about race in the first place.

"Either they're trying to identify more with one group or another, or they're trying to identify with both groups equally, or they want to imagine that they're, in some way, transcending racial boundaries altogether," Karl continued. "All of those make sense, and all of those are slightly problematic."

Ultimately, US Americans with mixed-race ancestry will still identify however they want based on a number of factors. In the essay "Black and Blue and Blond," for example, Thomas Chatterton Williams wrote that he never thought of himself as biracial or multiracial, even though he has both black and white ancestry: "One word I have never connected or been tempted to connect with is biracial." Instead, Thomas always thought of himself as just black.

Biracial writer Olivia Woldemikael also noted that Barack Obama, who has a black father and a white mother, is considered by most to be black rather than biracial. Noted in history as the first black president, Olivia writes that "Barack Obama made choices in his life that strengthened his connection with African Americans and bolstered his claim to American blackness: marrying the darker-skinned Michelle, organising (sic) in black communities of Chicago, checking 'black' on the census."

In contrast to Thomas and Barak, Olivia cites US American actress and English duchess Meghan Markle as an icon for biracial US Americans: "Her straightened hair, her mainstream American role on the television show, *Suits*, and her choice of husband—the whitest of Prince Charmings—allows Meghan Markle to edge towards whiteness," Olivia writes. "Instead of 'passing' or trying to hide her blackness, however, she is outspoken and exudes pride in her heritage. She insists that blackness is a stamp of honour (sic) rather than a stain on Windsor and has taught the American media a new word: biracial."

Of race in general, Karl said, the idea of race is closely related to the idea of inequality. If we can begin to deconstruct wealth disparities in the US, he believes, race will be that much easier to untangle.

"As long as social inequality exists, the idea of race is going to exist, because it's still useful as a way of trying to explain away that inequality," said Karl. "Intermarriage in and of itself isn't going to solve inequality."

Acknowledgements

WRITING A BOOK IS A long, terrifying, and wonderful process, and it is something I could not have done alone. I understand, now, why authors often have pages and pages of acknowledgements.

First, I need to thank Alanna Ramos, Andy Lowry, Cirleen DeBlaere, Clara Cardiello, Daniela Galimi, David Langton, David Pasteelnick, Delores Ng, Devon Murphy-Anderson, Elias Smolcic-Larson, Gillian Sherman, Helen Sheenan, Jae Langton, Jenna Lowry, José Moya, Joy Sheenan, Julian Humes, Karl Jacoby, Karl Stewart, Kazuhiro Gomi, Kristen Sheenan, Laura Generale, Layla Rafaoui, Leah Whetten-Goldstein, Lynda Gomi, Miranda Larbi, Nina Werbel Blauner, Rachael Langton, Shari Goldstein, Shelley Langton, Simone Thomas, and Trey Ellis for letting me into their lives, sharing their families with me, and/or taking the time to explain their research and how what they do affects every day lives. All of them helped me more than I can say here.

Thank you to Gwenda Blair for looking over the very rough first stages of a grad school thesis, and to Dale Maharidge,

Heather Hayton, Mylène Dressler, Nick Chiles, Rachael Marks, and Ray Hemachandra for always offering advice. To the English department at Guilford College for teaching me that you can use your words to make a difference, and also that words are really fun. It's a lesson I'll never forget. Thank you to Tiffany Moleski, my first real writing teacher. I'd like to think I've come a long way since we started.

Thank you to Julián Esteban Torres López and *The Nasiona* for publishing this book and "Jujubes Represent Sugar" as an excerpt, reaffirming that these are stories people need to read. Thank you to the readers of this book. Without you, I would just be writing for the sake of it.

Thank you to my amazing friends (you know who you are) for being nothing but supportive and assuaging my anxieties about publishing this book. Thank you to Elizabeth Houde, especially, for looking over the manuscript and making sure I had every comma in place.

Last, thank you to my supportive, crazy, loving family, Rachel Barnard and Sandi Zelniker. You've been reading my books since I was five years old and stapling the pages backwards. I hope it's paid off.

Bibliography

"15th Amendment to the U.S. Constitution." *Primary Documents of American History*, The Library of Congress, 27 June 2018.

"2010 Census Shows Multiple-Race Population Grew Faster Than Single-Race Population." *US Census Bureau Public Information Office*, The United States Government, 27 Sept. 2012.

"2018 SOC User Guide: FAQs and Acknowledgements." *U.S. Bureau of Labor Statistics*, The United States Government, Nov. 2017.

"5 Surprising Facts About Biracial Americans." *Mixed Remixed*, WordPress, 2 Feb. 2017.

"About Maccabi USA." *Maccabi USA*, WordPress.

"About Race." *US Census Bureau*, The United States Government, 23 Jan. 2018.

"Adopting a Child from China FAQs." *New Beginnings*, PCQB WordPress Support.

"Adopting a Child from Korea FAQs." *New Beginnings*, PCQB WordPress Support.

"Adopting as a Single Parent." *Child Welfare Information Gateway*, U.S. Department of Health and Human Services: Children's Bureau, Oct. 2013.

"Adoption in South Korea." *Adoption.com*, Elevati, LLC.

"Adoption Statistics." *U.S. Department of State*, U.S. Department of State.

"A Korean and Chinese Culture Camp." Edited by David Tiger, *Camp Friendship NJ*, 2004.

Asian American Federation of New York Census Information Center. "Ensus Profile: New York City's Asian American Population." *Asian American Federation*, New York Census Information Center, 2004.

Arnaz, Desi. *A Book*. New York: William Morrow, 1976.

Associated Press. "After 40 Years, Interracial Marriage Flourishing." *NBCNews*, NBCUniversal News Group, 15 Apr. 2007.

Barris, Kenya. "Black-Ish." Season one, episode one, ABC, 24 Sept. 2014.

Bates, Karen Grigsby. "Love In Technicolor: Interracial Families On Television." *NPR*, NPR, 15 Feb. 2014.

"Babson College." *College Simply*, U.S. Department of Education National Center for Education Statistics.

"Barnard College." *College Simply*, U.S. Department of Education National Center for Education Statistics.

Berman, Eliza. "Ghost in the Shell 2017 Controversy: A Comprehensive Guide." *Time*, Time Inc., 29 Mar. 2017.

Burmila, Edward. "The Democratic House Must Prioritize Protecting the 2020 Census." *The Nation*, The Nation Company LLC, 13 Nov. 2018.

Bérubé, A. (2001). How gay stays white and what kind of white it stays. In B. B. Rasmussen, E.

Klinenberg, I. J. Nexica, & M. Wray (Eds.), "The Making and Unmaking of Whiteness." Durham, NC: Duke University Press.

Bicks, Jenny and Bill Condon. "The Greatest Showman." 20 Dec. 2017.

Bonilla-Silva, E. (2000). "This is a White Country": The racial ideology of the Western nations of the world-system." Sociological Quarterly.

Boursaw, Jane Louise. "Fall TV." *Northern Express*, Way Back Machine, 2003.

"Bronxville, NY Demographic Data." *NeighborhoodScout*, Location, Inc.

Brooker, Charlie. "San Junipero." *Black Mirror*, season 3, episode 4, Netflix, 21 Oct. 2016.

Brown, Michael. "I Love Lucy, Miscegenation and Passing." *Interracial Relationships and the Media*, Wordpress, 10 Dec. 2011.

Brown, Michael. "The Jeffersons, Promoting Stereotypes?" *Interracial Relationships and the Media*, WordPress, 10 Dec. 2011.

Brown, Stacia L. "The Problem With Saying 'Black Babies Cost Less to Adopt'." *The Atlantic*, Atlantic Media Company, 1 July 2013.

Brown, Stephen Rex. "Mixed Race Becomes Second Fastest-Growing Racial Group in U.S." *NY Daily News*, NEW YORK DAILY NEWS, 23 June 2016.

"Bureau of Justice Statistics." Bureau of Justice Statistics (BJS), Office of Justice Programs.

Butler, Kiera. "Black People Are More Likely than Whites to Die of Heart Disease. Here's One Reason Why." *Mother Jones*, Mother Jones and the Foundation for National Progress, 13 June 2018.

Calacal, Celisa. "This Is How Many People Police Have Killed so Far in 2016." *ThinkProgress*, Word Press, 5 July 2016.

"Caucasian." *Merriam-Webster*, Merriam-Webster.

"Census Mapping Module: Dublin City." *All-Island Research Observatory*, Maynooth University, 2016.

Chanda, Rupa, and Sriparna Ghosh. "The Punjabi Diaspora in the UK: An Overview of Characteristics and Contributions to India." *European University Institute*, Aug. 2013.

Chatterton Williams, Thomas. "Black and Blue and Blond." *The Best American Essays*, edited by Robert Atwan and Jonathan Franzen, Houghton Mifflin, 2016, pp. 290–301.

Chatterton Williams, Thomas. "Thomas Chatterton Williams: My Black Privilege." *Los Angeles Times*, 3 Jan. 2016.

"China Heritage Journeys." *Adoptive Family Travel*, 2016, Comstar.biz.

Chong, Vanessa, "Racial Identity, Family, and Psychological Adjustment in Asian-White Biracial Young Adults" (2012). Electronic Theses and Dissertations. 4797.

Clehane, Diane. "The Chinese Adoption Effect." *Vanity Fair: The Hive*, Condé Nast, 18 Aug. 2008.

Collmeyer, Patricia M. "From 'Operation Brown Baby' to 'Opportunity': The Placement of Children of Color at the Boys and Girls Aid Society of Oregon." *Child Welfare*, vol. 74, no. 1, 1995. *ERIC.*

Craven, Julia. "More Than 250 Black People Were Killed By Police In 2016 [Updated]." *The Huffington Post*, Oath Inc., 1 Jan. 2017.

Crowe, Cameron. "Aloha." 27 May 2015.

"Crown Heights." *Point 2 Homes*, Onboard Informatics.

Cuddy, A. J. C., Fiske, S. T., & Glick, P. (2007). "The BIAS map: Behaviors from Intergroup Affect and Stereotypes." Journal of Personality and Social Psychology.

Davis, Arianna. "Why It's So Important Hollywood Is (Finally!) Normalizing Interracial Love." *Refinery29*, 10 Aug. 2017.

Delmont, Matthew. "TV's First Interracial Kiss Launched a Lifelong Career in Activism." *The Conversation US*, The Conversation, 3 Sept. 2018.

"Demographic Characteristics of the District and Metro Area." The Government of Washington, D.C., 2012, pp. 35-72.

Devos, T., & Banaji, M. R. (2005). "American = white?" Journal of Personality and Social Psychology, 88, 447-466.

Dimon, Laura. "19 Actual Statistics about America's Prison System." *Mic*, Mic Network Inc., 3 Apr. 2014.

"Dobbs Ferry, New York." *Fact Finder*, United States Census Bureau, 5 Oct. 2010.

Eberhardt, J. L., Davies, P. G., Purdie-Vaughns, V. J., & Johnson, S. L. (2006). "Looking Deathworthy: Perceived Stereotypicality of Black Defendants Predicts Capital-sentencing Outcomes." Psychological Science, 17, 383–386.

Eberhardt, J. L., Goff, P. A., Purdie, V. J., & Davies, P. G. (2004). "Seeing Black: Race, Crime, and Visual Processing." Journal of Personality and Social Psychology, 87, 876–963.

Economics and Statistics Administration. "2018 Census Test." *The United States Census Bureau*, The United States Government, 2018.

Ellen, Barbara. "Leona Lewis: 'I'm No Pushover!'." *The Guardian*, Guardian News and Media Limited, 24 Oct. 2009.

Ennis, Sharon R., et al. "The Hispanic Population: 2010." *United State Census Bureau*, United State Census Bureau, May 2011.

Equality Maps: Foster and Adoption Laws. Movement Advancement Project. Denver, CO.

"Fatal Force: 2018 Police Shootings Database." *The Washington Post*, WP Company, 2018.

"Financial Aid and Scholarships." *La Unidad Latina, Lambda Upsilon Lambda Fraternity, Inc.*, Lambda Upsilon Lambda Fraternity Inc.

Flores, Antonio. "Facts on Latinos in America." *Pew Research Center: Hispanic Trends*, The Pew Research Center, 18 Sept. 2017.

Fuentes, Jennice. "Jesse Williams Is Not Just a Pretty Face." *Global Grind*, Interactive One, LLC., 26 Jan. 2012.

Gates, Gary J., M.V. Lee Badgett, Kate Chambers and Jennifer Macomber. "Adoption and Foster Care by Gay and Lesbian

Parents in the United States." The Williams Institute, Los Angeles, CA. 2007.

"Gay and Lesbian Adoption Laws." *Findlaw,* Thomson Reuters, 2018.

Gillette, William. *The Right to Vote: Politics and the Passage of the Fifteenth Amendment.* Baltimore: Johns Hopkins Press, 1969.

Gleiberman, Owen. "'The Hate U Give': A Racial Drama So Honest Every American Should See It." *Variety,* Penske Business Media, LLC., 21 Oct. 2018.

Goldberg, Lesley. "'Black-Ish' Spinoff 'Grown-Ish' Renewed at Freeform." *The Hollywood Reporter,* 18 Jan. 2018.

Goodloe, J. Mills, and Nicola Yoon. "Everything, Everything." 19 May 2017.

Gonzalez-Barrera, Ana, and Mark Hugo Lopez. "Spanish Is the Most Spoken Non-English Language in U.S. Homes, Even among Non-Hispanics." *Fact Tank,* Pew Research Center, 13 Aug. 2013.

González , Juan, and Amy Goodman. "Jailed for Life for Stealing a $159 Jacket? 3,200 Serving Life without Parole for Nonviolent Crimes." *Democracy Now!,* 15 Nov. 2013.

Goodstein, Laurie. "Poll Shows Major Shift in Identity of U.S. Jews." *The New York Times,* 1 Oct. 2013.

Gordon, Emily V., and Kumail Nanjiani. "The Big Sick." 23 June 2017.

Greig, Astrea. "Seven Essential Facts about Multiracial Youth." *American Psychological Association,* Aug. 2013.

Grey's Anatomy. Created by Shonda Rhimes, ABC, 27 March 2005.

Hall, Loretta. "Iroquois Confederacy." *Countries and Their Cultures*, Every Culture.

Hancock, A. M. (2007). "When Multiplication Doesn't Equal Quick Addition: Examining Intersectionality As a Research Paradigm." Perspectives on Politics, 5, 63–79.

Harriot, Michael. "Here's How Many People Police Killed in 2017." *The Root*, Gizmodo Media Group, 2 Jan. 2018.

"Hartsdale, New York." *Fact Finder*, United States Census Bureau, 5 Oct. 2010.

Hay, Jeff, ed. *Amendment XV: Race and the Right to Vote*. Farmington Hills, Mich: Greenhaven Press, 2009.

"How Does Babson College Rank Among America's Best Colleges?" *U.S. News & World Report*, U.S. News & World Report L.P.

"How Many Couples Are Waiting to Adopt?" *American Adoptions*.

"International Adoption: Health Guidance and the Immigration Process." *Immigrant and Refugee Health*, Centers for Disease Control and Prevention, 8 Jan. 2018.

Jackson, Cheryl, and Michael Cromartie. "Religion and Race: A Historical and Contemporary Perspective." *Pew Research Center's Religion & Public Life Project*, The Pew Charitable Trusts, 8 Dec. 2008.

"JAMAICA." *The World Factbook*, Central Intelligence Agency.

Jane the Virgin. Created by Jennie Snyder Urman, The CW, 13 Oct. 2014.

Johnson, Kay Ann. "China's Hidden Children: Abandonment, Adoption, and the Human Costs of the One-Child Policy." The University of Chicago Press, 2017.

Jeffries, V., & Ransford, H. E. (1980). *Social Stratification: A Multiple Hierarchy Approach*. Boston: Allyn & Bacon.

Jones, Nicholas A., and Jungmiwha Bullock. "The Two or More Races Population: 2010." *United States Census Bureau*, U.S. Department of Commerce, Sept. 2012.

"Jose Moya, Barnard College History Professor." *Daily Motion*, 2015.

"Jose Moya." *The Heyman Center*, Columbia University.

Joyce, Kathryn. "The Threat of International Adoption for Migrant Children Separated From Their Families." *The Intercept*, First Look Media, 1 July 2018.

Joyce, Kathryn. "The Truth about China's Missing Daughters." *The New Republic*, 1 June 2016.

Karlin, Lily. "Why Lucille Ball Was More Revolutionary Than You Think." *The Huffington Post*, Oath Inc., 26 Apr. 2015.

Karuga, James. "US States With The Largest Relative African-American Populations." *WorldAtlas*, 25 Apr. 2017.

"Keene, New Hampshire." *Fact Finder*, United States Census Bureau, 5 Oct. 2010.

Keesee, Tracie. "Equity and Inclusion." *Bureaus*, New York Police Department.

Keller, Larry. "New White Supremacist Party Has Mass Electoral Ambitions." *Southern Poverty Law Center*, 30 May 2010.

Khabeer, Suad Abdul. "Trump's Muslim Ban Is a Dangerous Distraction." *Al Jazeera*, Al Jazeera, 29 Jan. 2017.

Kim, Eleana. Adopted Territory: Transnational Korean Adoptees and the Politics of Belonging. Duke University Press, 2011.

Kohli, Ritu. "US States With The Largest Relative Asian American Populations." *WorldAtlas*, 25 Apr. 2017.

Kreider, Rose M. "Adopted Children and Stepchildren: 2000." United State Census Bureau, Oct. 2003.

La Jeunesse, Marilyn. "10 Movies That Have Been Accused of Whitewashing." *Business Insider*, Insider Inc., 26 Sept. 2018.

Lama, Abraham. "'Home' Is Where the Heartbreak Is for Japanese-Peruvians." *Asia Times*, Asia Times Online Co., Ltd., 16 Oct. 1999.

Landrine, H., Klonoff, E. A., Alcaraz, R., Scott, J., & Wilkins, P. (1995). "Multiple Variables in Discrimination." In B. Lott & D. Maluso (Eds.), *The Social Psychology of Interpersonal Discrimination*. New York: Guilford Press.

Langan, Patrick A. "The Racial Disparity in U.S. Drug Arrests." *Bureau of Justice Statistics*, U.S. Department of Justice, 1 Oct. 1995.

Larbi, Miranda. "Having Mixed Race Kids Doesn't Mean You're Woke." *Metro*, Associated NewspapersLimited, 24 Oct. 2017, 5:28 p.m.

"Latinos in America: A Demographic Overview." *American Immigration Council*, The American Immigration Council, 29 Apr. 2012.

Leah, Rachel. "U.S. Police Killed 1,129 People in 2017, but That's Not the Full Body Count." *Salon*, Salon Media Group, Inc., 7 Jan. 2018.

Lee, Elizabeth, and John Smith. "Numbers of Mixed-Race Americans Growing." Edited by George Grow, *Let's Learn English*, VOA, 11 Mar. 2017.

Lee, Richard M., et al. "Cultural Socialization in Families with Internationally Adopted Children." *Journal of Family Psychology*, vol. 20, no. 4, 2006, pp. 571–580.

Levin, S., Sinclair, S., Veniegas, R. C., & Taylor, P. L. (2002). "Perceived Discrimination in the Context of Multiple Group Memberships." *Psychological Science*.

"LGBT Adoption Statistics." *LifeLong Adoptions*, 2018.

Lien, P. (1994). "Ethnicity and Political Participation: A Comparison Between Asian and Mexican Americans." *Political Behavior*.

Livingston, Gretchen. "The Rise of Multiracial and Multiethnic Babies in the U.S." *Fact Tank*, Pew Research Center, 6 June 2017.

"Loving v. Virginia." *Findlaw*, Thomson Reuters.

"Loving v. Virginia." *Oyez*, 29 Sep. 2018.

"Lucille Ball Biography." *Killer Media*, Way Back Machine, 2 Jan. 2017.

Mabrey, Salendria. "Human Discount: Why Do Black Children Cost Less to Adopt?" *Foster Care Newsletter*, 1 Sept. 2016.

Maddox, K. B. (2004). "Perspectives on Racial Phenotypicality Bias." *Personality and Social Psychology Review*.

Malik, Sanam. "Asian Immigrants in the United States Today." *Center for American Progress*, 21 May 2015, 9:07 a.m.

Martin, Michel. "Should Kids See 'The Hunger Games'?" *Special Series: Parenting*, National Public Radio, 3 Apr. 2012.

McCall, L. (2005). "The Complexity of Intersectionality." Signs.

McNary, Dave. "'Riverdale' Star K.J. Apa Replaces Kian Lawley in 'The Hate U Give' Movie." *Variety*, Penske Business Media, LLC., 3 Apr. 2018.

McRoy, Ruth G., et al. "Self-Esteem and Racial Identity in Transracial and Inracial Adoptees." *Social Work*, vol. 27, no. 6, 1 Nov. 1982, pp. 522–526. *NASW Press.*

"Median Household Income in the Past 12 Months (in 2016 inflation-adjusted dollars)." *American Community Survey.* United States Census Bureau. 2016.

"Metropolitan and Micropolitan." *US Census Bureau*, The United States Government, 22 Mar. 2017.

Modern Family. Created by Steven Levitan, and Christopher Lloyd, ABC, 23 Sept. 2009.

Mohamed, Besheer. "A New Estimate of the U.S. Muslim Population." *Fact Tank*, Pew Research Center, 6 Jan. 2016.

Martohardjono, Zavé, et al. "Mass Incarceration: An Animated Series." *American Civil Liberties Union*, The American Civil Liberties Union Foundation., 2018.

Moss, Jamie, William Wheeler and Ehren Kruger. "Ghost in the Shell." 16 March 2017.

"Multiracial in America: Proud, Diverse and Growing in Numbers." *Pew Research Center's*

Social & Demographic Trends Project, The Pew Research Center, 11 June 2015.

Murphy, Caryle. "Interfaith Marriage Is Common in U.S., Particularly among the Recently Wed." *Pew Research Center,* The Pew Charitable Trusts, 2 June 2015.

"New York." *American FactFinder,* United State Census Bureau, 5 Oct. 2010.

"New York Republican U.S. Rep. Peter King Re-Elected to 14th Term With Victory Over Democrat Liuba Grechen Shirley." *U.S. News & World Report,* The Associated Press, 7 Nov. 2018, 12:55 a.m.

Nicholson, David. "Jesse Williams Learns and Plays History." *The Daily Press,* Tribune Publishing Company, 18 Sept. 2010.

Nittle, Nadra Kareem. "Interracial Couples on TV Shows in the 20th Century." *ThoughtCo,* Dotdash, 12 Apr. 2018.

Nittle, Nadra Kareem. "The Roots of Colorism, or Skin Tone Discrimination." *ThoughtCo,* Dotdash, 22 July 2018.

NPR Staff. "Six Words: 'Black Babies Cost Less to Adopt'." *NPR,* 27 June 2013.

Ordoña, Michael. "Zac Efron and Zendaya Bring Romance, and a Standout Duet, to 'The Greatest Showman'." *Los Angeles Times,* 19 Dec. 2017.

O'Rourke, Jill. "7 Great TV Shows With Adoption Storylines You Can Watch Right Now." *A Plus,* Chicken Soup for the Soul, 14 Nov. 2017.

"Our Camp China." *Our Camp China.*

Overview of Lesbian and Gay Parenting, Adoption and Foster Care. American Civil Liberties Union, New York, NY.

Oyiboke, Amen. "'Everything, Everything's Interracial Romance Matters So Much." *Bustle*, 16 May 2017.

Pace, James O. *Amendment to the Constitution: Averting the Decline and Fall of America.* Johnson, Pace, Simmons, & Fennell, 1986.

Parvin, Ellie. "Fortune Cookie US Invention." *Golden Gater Online*, Way Back Machine, 31 Jan. 1995.

Pastor, Pam. "Deric McCabe's Message to Filipinos: I'm Proud to Be Filipino and to Represent Them." *Lifestyle*, The Inquirer, 11 Mar. 2018, 5:15 a.m.

"Persons Seeking to Adopt." *Administration for Children and Families*, U.S. Department of Health and Human Services, 13 Nov. 2002.

"Peter King." *Islamophobia*, The Counter Islamophobia Project, 5 Oct. 2017.

"Population: North America: Counting Jews of Color in the U.S." *Be'chol Lashon*, Global Jews

"Population, Total." *The World Bank*, The World Bank Group, 2018.

Portée, Alex. "Gina Rodriguez Does Salsa For Puerto Rican Relief On Ellen Show." *Fierce*, We Are Mitú, 12 Oct. 2017.

Purdie-Vaughns, Valerie, and Richard P. Eibach. "Intersectional Invisibility: The Distinctive Advantages and Disadvantages of Multiple Subordinate-Group Identities." *Columbia University*, Springer Science + Business Media, LLC 2008, 2008.

Quah, Nicholas, and Laura E. Davis. "Here's A Timeline Of Unarmed Black People Killed By Police Over Past Year." *BuzzFeed News*, BuzzFeed, 1 May 2015.

"Questions and Answers for Census 2000 Data on Race." *U.S. Census Bureau*, The United States Government, 14 Mar. 2001.

Quinn, Jill Sisson. "Big Night." *The Best American Essays*, edited by Robert Atwan and Jonathan Franzen, Houghton Mifflin, 2016, pp. 213-230.

"Race and Ethnicity: Clues to Your Heart Disease Risk?" *Harvard Health Blog*, Harvard Health Publishing, 17 July 2015.

"Racial Disparities in Nationally Notifiable Diseases." *Centers for Disease Control and Prevention*, United States Government, 14 Jan. 2005.

"Raising Both Adopted and Biological Children." *America's Adoption Agency*, American Adoptions.

"Reality Check: Who Voted for Donald Trump?" *BBC News*, BBC, 9 Nov. 2016.

Reaves, Brian A. "Local Police Departments, 2013: Personnel, Policies, and Practices." *Bureau of Justice Statistics (BJS)*, U.S. Department of Justice, May 2015.

"Reform Myths." American Adoption Congress, MemberLeap.

Reilly, Mollie. "Same-Sex Couples Can Now Adopt Children In All 50 States." *The Huffington Post*, Oath Inc., 31 Mar. 2016.

"Revisions to the Standards for the Classification of Federal Data on Race and Ethnicity." *The White House: President Barack Obama*, National Archives and Records Administration, 30 Oct. 1997.

Roberts, Dorothy E. "Shattered Bonds: The Color of Child Welfare." RHYW, 2010.

Runcie, Ayanna. "As New York's Asian-American Population Grows, Government Grants Lag Behind." *NBCNews*, NBCUniversal News Group, 7 Mar. 2017.

Saul, Josh. "Police Killed More than 1,100 People This Year and a Quarter of Them Were Black." *Newsweek*, NEWSWEEK LLC, 29 Dec. 2017.

Savage, Charlie. "Justice Dept. Seeks to Curtail Stiff Drug Sentences." *The New York Times*, 12 Aug. 2013.

Schabner, Dean. "Why It Costs More to Adopt a White Baby." *ABC News*, ABC News Network, 12 Mar. 2018.

"Scotch Plains Township." *American FactFinder*, Data Access and Dissemination Systems, 5 Oct. 2010.

Simon, Jeff. "Donald Trump Impersonates Asian Negotiators." *CNN Politics*, Turner Broadcasting System, Inc., 26 Aug. 2015.

Smith, Nigel M. "Emma Stone Says Aloha Casting Taught Her about Whitewashing in Hollywood." *The Guardian*, Guardian News and Media Limited, 17 July 2015.

"St. Thomas More School Profile." *Boarding School Review*, Boarding School Review LLC, 2018.

"St. Thomas More School." *St. Thomas More School*, Blackboard Inc., 2002.

Staat, Mary Allen, and Heather Burke. "International Travel with Infants & Children." *Travelers' Health*, Centers for Disease Control and Prevention, 12 June 2017.

Steiner, George. "The Eleventh Commandment." *The Best American Essays*, edited by Robert Atwan and Jonathan Franzen, Houghton Mifflin, 2016, pp. 260-273.

Stenberg, Amandla. "Amandla Stenberg: 'So Excited to Be Playing Rue in the Hunger Games.'" *Svensk Hungerspelen Fansida*, Hunger-Games.Net, 20 Apr. 2011.

Stern, Claire. "7 Things You May Not Know About Black-Ish Star Yara Shahidi." *InStyle*, Meredith Beauty Group, 23 Apr. 2015.

Stewart, Carolyn. "Census of Population and Housing." U.S. Census Bureau Publications Census of Population and Housing, United States Census Bureau, 19 Aug. 2011.

"Student Population at Muhlenberg College." *College Tuition Compare*, 2017.

Sue, S. "Science, ethnicity, and bias: Where Have We Gone Wrong?" *American Psychologist*, 1999.

Takeda , Allison. "Zendaya Digs Deep Into Her Past for Immigrant Heritage Month." *Us Weekly*, Wenner Media, 9 June 2015.

"Tay-Sachs Disease." *U.S. National Library of Medicine*, National Institutes of Health, 2 Oct. 2018.

"*The Bronze Bride* (1917)." *IMDb*, Amazon.

"The Constitution: Amendments 11-27." *National Archives*, The U.S. National Archives and Records Administration, 6 Oct. 2016.

"The Counted: Tracking People Killed by Police in the United States | US News." *The Guardian*, Guardian News and Media.

The Fosters. Created by Bradley Bredeweg and Peter Paige, Freeform, 3 June 2013.

This is Us. Created by Dan Fogelman, NBC, 20 Sept. 2016.

Thompson, Irene. "Cantonese." *About World Languages*, The Technology Development Group, 29 May 2015.

Thompson, Irene. "Mandarin." *About World Languages*, The Technology Development Group, 12 May 2017.

"Transracial Adoption: Expert Advice If You're Adopting Transracially." *An Open Adoption Meeting Place*, America Adopts, 26 July 2013.

"Trinity College." *College Simply*, U.S. Department of Education National Center for Education Statistics.

Truffaut-Wong, Olivia. "Gugu Mbatha-Raw Is Changing Hollywood." *Bustle*, 6 Apr. 2016.

"Undergraduate Ethnic Diversity at Boston University." *College Factual*, Media Factual.

"Undergraduate Ethnic Diversity at Case Western University." *College Factual*, Media Factual.

"Undergraduate Ethnic Diversity at Carlton College." *College Factual*, Media Factual.

"Undergraduate Ethnic Diversity at Cornell University." *College Factual*, Media Factual.

"Undergraduate Ethnic Diversity at George Washington University." *College Factual*, Media Factual.

"Undergraduate Ethnic Diversity at Guilford College." *College Factual*, Media Factual.

"Undergraduate Ethnic Diversity at Keene State College." *College Factual*, Media Factual.

"Undergraduate Ethnic Diversity at Georgia State University." *College Factual*, Media Factual.

United States Census Bureau. "Demographic Trends." census.gov. 11 Oct. 2010.

"U.S. and World Population Clock." *Population Clock*, United States Census Bureau.

U.S. Census Bureau. 2010 Census Briefs.

U.S. Department of Commerce. Statistical Abstract of the United States. United States Census Bureau, 2006.

Varagur, Krithika. "Really? Congressman Peter King Uses Anti-Asian Slur On TV." *The Huffington Post*, Oath Inc., 14 May 2016, 4:42 p.m.

Vile, John R. "Pace, James O. (1954-)." Encyclopedia of Constitutional Amendments, 1996, p. 337.

"Vision: A Global Jewish People." *Be'chol Lashon*, Global Jews.

Vital Statistics in Japan. Ministry of Health, Labour and Welfare.

Wagner, Jayce. "White Supremacist Trump Delegate Wants To Deport Mixed Race Americans." *The Inquisitr*, The Inquisitr, 10 May 2016.

Waldmeir, Patti. "Adopting an Abandoned Chinese Baby: A Family's Experience." *Financial Times*, The Nikkei, 25 July 2014.

Wang, Hansi Lo. "2020 Census Will Ask Black People About Their Exact Origins." *All Things Considered*, National Public Radio, 13 Mar. 2018.

Wang, Hansi Lo. "2020 Census Will Ask White People More About Their Ethnicities." *All Things Considered*, National Public Radio, 1 Feb. 2018.

Wang, Wendy. "Interracial Marriage: Who Is 'Marrying Out'?" *Fact Tank*, Pew Research Center, 12 June 2015.

Wardlow, Ciara. "The Idealized Diversity of 'A Wrinkle in Time'." *The Hollywood Reporter*, 9 Mar. 2018.

"We Are Spence-Chapin." *Spence-Chapin*, Spence-Chapin Services to Families and Children.

Wells, Audrey. "The Hate U Give" 5 Oct. 2018.

"What Are a Birth Mother's Rights Regarding Adoption?" *Adoption Services, Inc.*, Our Adoption Agency.

Wickes, Kevin L., and John R. Slate. "Transracial Adoption of Koreans: A Preliminary Study of Adjustment." *International Journal for the Advancement of Counselling*, vol. 19, no. 2, 1997, pp. 187–195.

Woldemikael, Olivia. "Why Barack Is Black and Megan Is Biracial." *Media Diversified*, WordPress, 28 June 2018.

Wolfe, Brendan. "Racial Integrity Laws (1924–1930)." *Encyclopedia Virginia*, Virginia Foundation for the Humanities, 17 Feb. 2009.

Wormald, Benjamin. "Muslims Views on Interfaith Relations." *Pew Research Center's Religion & Public Life Project*, The Pew Charitable Trusts, 9 Jan. 2015.

Yam, Kimberly. "After Trump Deemed China Foreign Enemy, Anti-Asian Hate Crimes In LA Surged: Expert." *The Huffington Post*, Oath, Inc., 27 Jan. 2017.

Younge, Gary. "30% Of Black Men in US Will Go to Jail." *The Guardian*, Guardian News and Media, 18 Aug. 2003.

Zelniker, Nicole. "Alanna Ramos and Simone Thomas" 17 July 2018.

Zelniker, Nicole. "Cirleen DeBlaere." 25 Nov. 2017.

Zelniker, Nicole. "David Pasteelnick and Karl Stewart." 2 July 2018.

Zelniker, Nicole. "Elias Smolcic-Larson." 8 Nov. 2017.

Zelniker, Nicole. "Gillian Sherman." 27 Dec. 2017.

Zelniker, Nicole. "José Moya." 29 Nov. 2017.

Zelniker, Nicole. "Karl Jacoby." 4 Dec. 2017.

Zelniker, Nicole. "Laura Generale." 27 Jan. 2018.

Zelniker, Nicole. "Layla Rafaoui." 20 Nov. 2017.

Zelniker, Nicole. "Leah Whetten-Goldstein." 22 Nov. 2017.

Zelniker, Nicole. "Miranda Larbi." 2 Nov. 2017.

Zelniker, Nicole. "Nina Werbel Blauner." 17 July 2018.

Zelniker, Nicole. "Shari Goldstein." 25 Nov. 2017.

Zelniker, Nicole. "The Galimi Family." 18 Dec. 2017.

Zelniker, Nicole. "The Gomi Family." 17 Dec. 2017.

Zelniker, Nicole. "The Langton Family." 10 Dec. 2017.

Zelniker, Nicole. "The Ng Lowry Family." 9 Dec. 2017.

Zelniker, Nicole. "The Sheenan Family." 1 Jan. 2018.

Zelniker, Nicole. "Trey Ellis." 4 Dec. 2017.

Zhong, Fan. "Mackenzie Davis." *On the Verge*, W Magazine, 12 Mar. 2013.

Zong, Jie, and Jeanne Batalova. "Asian Immigrants in the United States." *Migration Policy Institute*, 6 Jan. 2016.

Zong, Jie, and Jeanne Batalova. "College-Educated Immigrants in the United States." *Migration Policy Institute*, 3 Feb. 2016.

About the Author

Nicole Zelniker is a graduate of the Columbia Journalism School and an editorial researcher with The Conversation US. Her work has appeared on The Pulitzer Prizes website and in *USA Today* and *Yes! Weekly*, among other places. A creative writer as well as a journalist, Nicole has had several pieces of poetry published including "Cracks in the Sidewalk" (*Quail Bell Magazine*) and "Surge" (*The Greenleaf Review*), as well as three short stories, "Last Dance" (*The Hungry Chimera*), "Dress Rehearsal" (*littledeathlit*), and "Lucky" (*Fixional*). You can check out the rest of her work at nicolezelniker.wordpress.com.

About *The Nasiona*

Birds then came, bringing in **seeds***, and our pile became an oasis of life.*

Pojawiły się ptaki, przynosząc **nasiona** *i nasza skądinąd jałowa górka stała się oazą życia. (Polish)*

The Nasiona is a community of creatives whose mission is to cultivate the seeds of nonfiction. We do this through a nonfiction literary magazine, podcast, and publishing house, as well as by offering editing services, literary contests, and an internship program.

In an age when telling the difference between reality and delusion is frighteningly labyrinthine, we focus on creative works based on facts, truth-seeking, human concerns, real events, and real people, with a personal touch.

From liminal lives to the marginalized, and everything in between, we glimpse into different, at times extraordinary, worlds to promote narrative-led nonfiction stories and art that explore the spectrum of human experience. We believe that the subjective can offer its own reality and reveal truths some facts can't discover.

We're a diversity-friendly organization that values multicultural and multi-experience perspectives on what it means to be human. We look to erase borders, tackle taboos, resist conventions, explore the known and unknown, and rename ourselves to claim ourselves.

We feature creative nonfiction and nonfiction poetry, book excerpts, a column on memoir writing, visual art, and interview interesting individuals from all over.

We publish continuously, on a rolling basis, and accept submissions from emerging and established authors and content creators.

We offer editing services for poetry, fiction, and nonfiction manuscripts of any length.

Our publishing house will begin publishing nonfiction book-length manuscripts in 2019.

Our internship program aims to contribute to the development of editors, journalists, writers, scholars, and those interested in the publishing industry.

With our literary contests, we look to identify and celebrate some of the best original, unpublished creative nonfiction and nonfiction poetry out there.

We founded *The Nasiona* in the summer of 2018 in California. Though based in hilly San Francisco, the world is our home. Help us cultivate this pile of seeds and we'll do our best to create a worthy oasis for human life to not only exist but flourish.

The Nasiona depends on voluntary contributions from readers like you. We hope the value of our work to the community is worth your patronage. If you like what we do, please show this by financially supporting our work through our Patreon platform.

https://www.patreon.com/join/TheNasiona

Please follow *The Nasiona* on Twitter, Instagram, and Facebook for regular updates: @TheNasiona

nasiona.mail@gmail.com

https://thenasiona.com/

CPSIA information can be obtained
at www.ICGtesting.com
Printed in the USA
LVHW052359310719
626123LV00007B/60/P